A CONSTELLATION OF ORIGAMI POLYHEDRA

A CONSTELLATION OF ORIGAMI POLYHEDRA

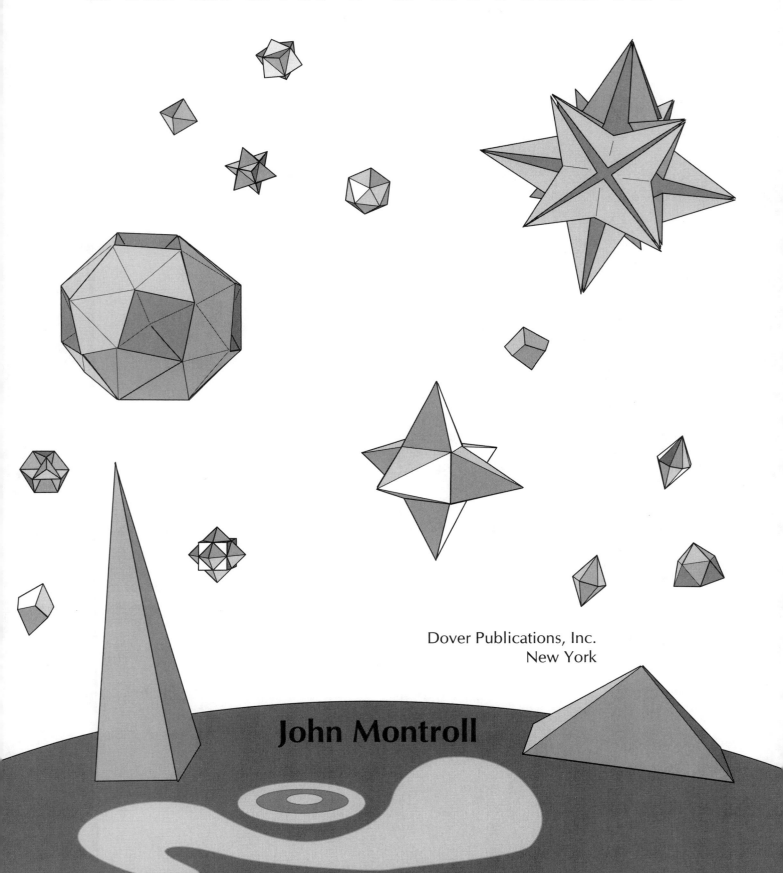

Dover Publications, Inc.
New York

John Montroll

To Robbie

Bibliographical Note

This work is first published in 2004 in separate editions by
Antroll Publishing Company, Maryland, and Dover Publications,
Inc., New York.

Library of Congress Cataloging-in-Publication Data

Montroll, John.
    A constellation of origami polyhedra / John Montroll.
       p. cm.
     ISBN 0-486-43958-5 (pbk.)
     1. Origami. 2.Polyhedra in art.   I. Title.
   TT870.M55323 2004
   736'.982—dc22

                                                              2004056139

          Manufactured in the United States of America
Dover Publications, Inc., 31 East 2nd Street, Mineola, N.Y. 11501

Introduction

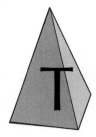

Throughout the ages, polyhedra have inspired several cultures with their beauty and mystery. It is very rewarding to capture these shapes through origami. I am pleased to present this sequel to *A Plethora of Polyhedra in Origami* which offers yet more projects for folders of all levels.

From the earthly pyramids to the stars, from diamonds to antidiamonds, this collection continues the journey into the secrets of polyhedra. Along the way are the eight deltahedra, square antiprism, and some sunken shapes. Each of these follow the familiar origami style of using a single square sheet of paper. Each model is accompanied with text and a crease pattern diagram, showing a two-dimensional layout. There is additional information on the forms of symmetry used for the folding methods.

The models are grouped into sections of related polyhedra and the groups become progressively more difficult. The illustrations conform to the internationally accepted Randlett-Yoshizawa conventions. The colored side of origami paper is represented by the shadings in the diagrams. Origami paper can be found in many hobby shops or purchased by mail from OrigamiUSA, 15 West 77th Street, New York, NY 10024-5192 or from Dover Publications, Inc., 31 East 2nd Street, Mineola, NY 11501. Large sheets are easier to use than small ones.

Many people helped with this project. I thank Charles Steelman for his ideas for the cover design. I thank Robert Lang for his efficient folding sequences. Thanks to John Szinger for his help with the text and continued support. Thanks to my editors, Jan Polish and Charley Montroll. And I also thank the many folders who proof read the diagrams.

John Montroll

Contents

★ Simple
★★ Intermediate
★★★ Complex
★★★★ Very Complex

Pyramids   *page 11*

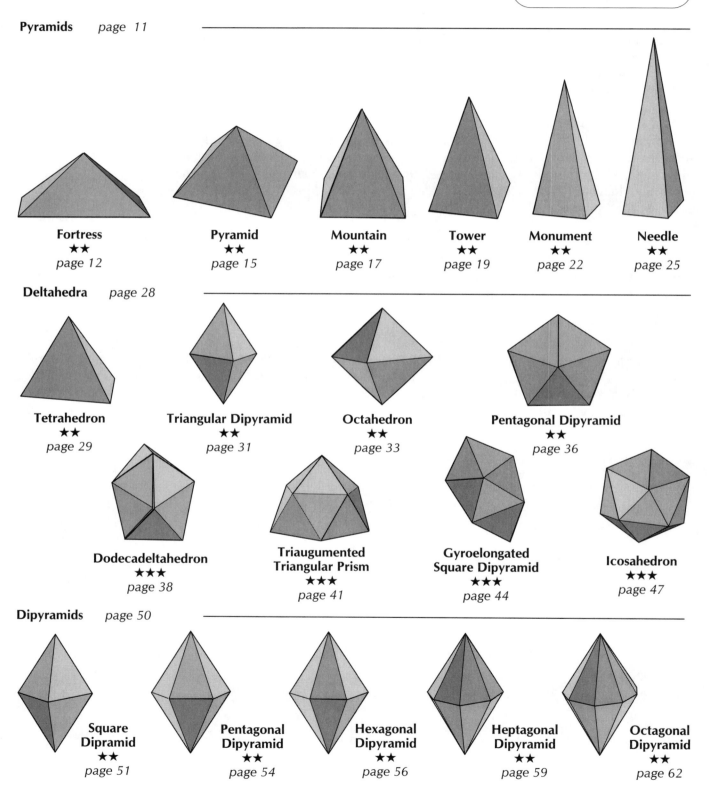

Fortress
★★
page 12

Pyramid
★★
page 15

Mountain
★★
page 17

Tower
★★
page 19

Monument
★★
page 22

Needle
★★
page 25

Deltahedra   *page 28*

Tetrahedron
★★
page 29

Triangular Dipyramid
★★
page 31

Octahedron
★★
page 33

Pentagonal Dipyramid
★★
page 36

Dodecadeltahedron
★★★
page 38

Triaugumented Triangular Prism
★★★
page 41

Gyroelongated Square Dipyramid
★★★
page 44

Icosahedron
★★★
page 47

Dipyramids   *page 50*

Square Dipramid
★★
page 51

Pentagonal Dipyramid
★★
page 54

Hexagonal Dipyramid
★★
page 56

Heptagonal Dipyramid
★★
page 59

Octagonal Dipyramid
★★
page 62

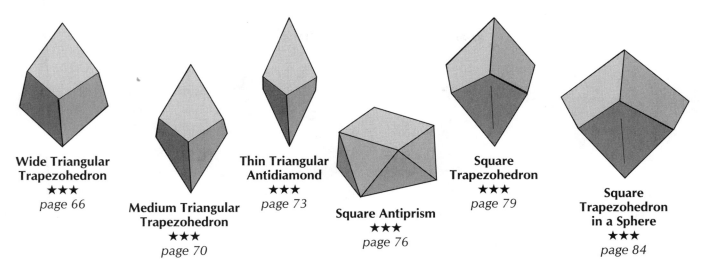
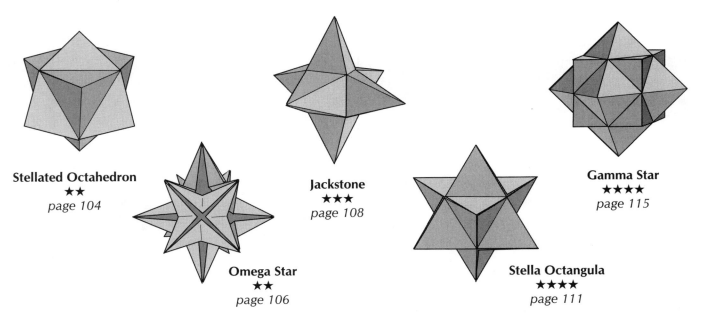

Symbols

Lines

— — — — — — — — — —   Valley fold, fold in front.

— · — · · — · — · · — · — · —   Mountain fold, fold behind.

————————————   Crease line.

·······································   X-ray or guide line.

Arrows

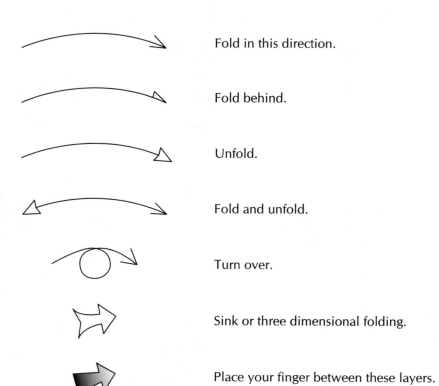

Fold in this direction.

Fold behind.

Unfold.

Fold and unfold.

Turn over.

Sink or three dimensional folding.

Place your finger between these layers.

Basic Folds

Squash Fold.
In a squash fold, some paper is opened and then made flat. The shaded arrow shows where to place your finger.

1
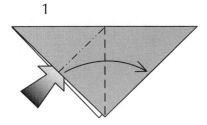

Squash-fold.

2
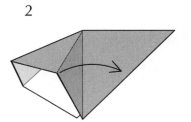

A three-dimensional intermediate step.

3
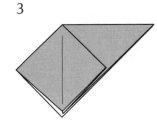

Inside Reverse Fold.
In an inside reverse fold, some paper is folded between layers. Here are two examples.

1
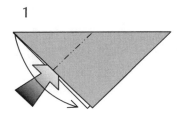

Reverse-fold.

2
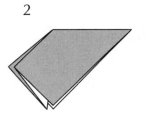

1

2

Reverse-fold.

Sink Fold.
In a sink fold, some of the paper without edges is folded inside. To do this fold, much of the model must be unfolded.

1
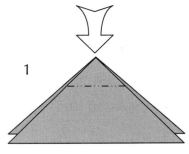

Sink.

2

Symmetry & Reference Finder

All the polyhedra in this collection have crease and folding patterns with certain symmetries. Symmetry simplifies the folding. The types used are—even, odd, even/odd, and square symmetry.

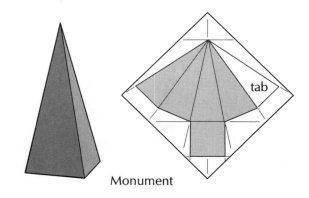

Even Symmetry

If the square is divided in half, the creases on each side are mirror images of each other. For some models, the tab can be treated as a side to maintain even symmetry. This form is used in the pyramids.

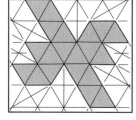

Monument

Odd Symmetry

The crease pattern is the same when rotated 180°. This common form is used for most of the deltahedra and antidiamonds.

Icosahedron

Even/odd Symmetry

The crease pattern is both even and odd. This is used for the diamonds. The tabs, however follow odd symmetry.

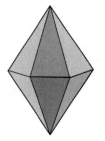
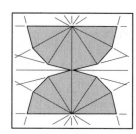

Hexagonal Dipyramid

Square Symmetry

The crease pattern is the same when rotated 90°. Since the square itself has this symmetry, it is an efficient method. It especially simplifies the folding since you only need to know one-fourth of the folding. This symmetry is used in the sunken shapes and stars.

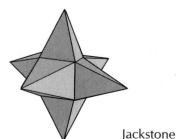
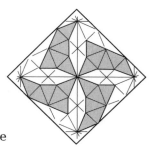

Jackstone

Reference Finder

Many models in this collection divide the paper into particular proportions not commonly found in traditional origami. In many cases, a series of folds will end in locating a landmark that becomes the key point to develop the geometry of the model. For many cases, I have used Robert Lang's Reference Finder software which finds a folding sequence to locate such points.

Pyramids

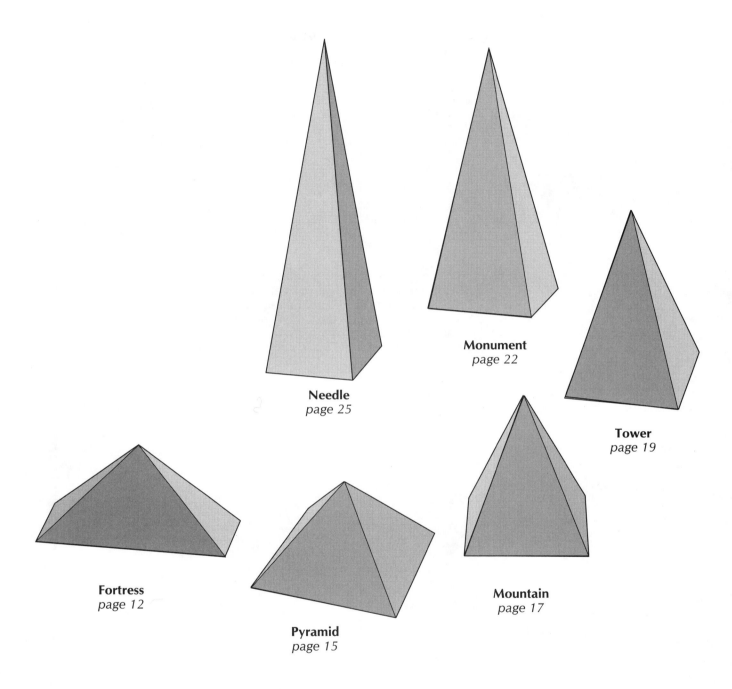

Needle
page 25

Monument
page 22

Tower
page 19

Fortress
page 12

Pyramid
page 15

Mountain
page 17

Some cultures believe the shape of a pyramid has special powers. This collection of square pyramids goes from short and squat to tall and thin. It makes for an interesting display when each is folded from the same size paper.

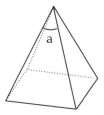

Pyramid	Angle a
Fortress	72°
Pyramid	60°
Mountain	45°
Tower	30°
Monument	22.5°
Needle	15°

Fortress

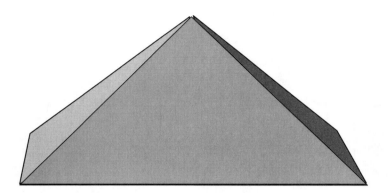

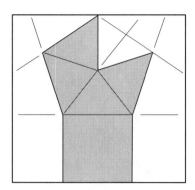

This stout pyramid is formed from a square base and four of five parts of a pentagon, with an apex angle of 72°. The crease pattern shows a pentagon above a square. The line between the two is formed in step 5. The line is located by following a folding sequence which was determined using Robert Lang's Reference Finder software.

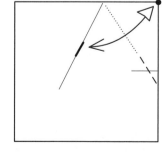

1

Fold and unfold on the right.

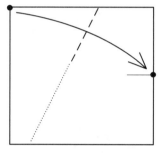

2

Fold at the top creasing lightly.

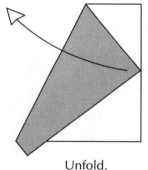

3

Unfold.

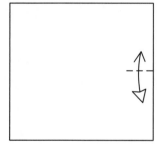

4

Fold and unfold to the line, creasing only at the right.

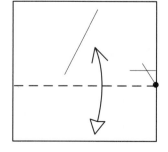

5

Fold and unfold.

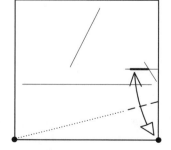

6

Fold and unfold bringing the bottom right corner to the line, creasing only on the right.

7

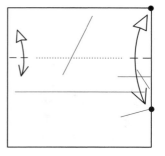

Fold and unfold on
the left and right.

8

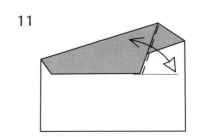

Fold and unfold.

9

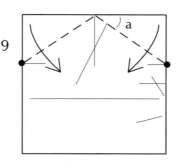

Angle a is
approximately 36°.

10

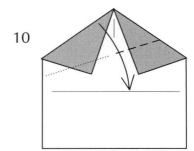

Fold to the line,
creasing on the right.

11

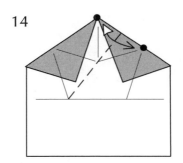

Fold and unfold.

12

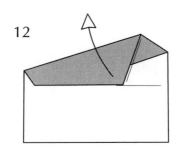

Unfold.

13

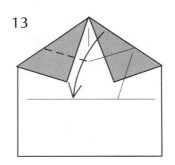

Repeat steps 10–12
on the other side.

14

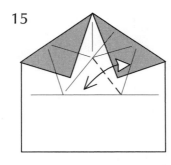

Fold and unfold.

15

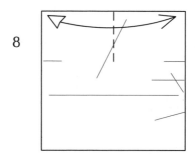

Fold and unfold.

16

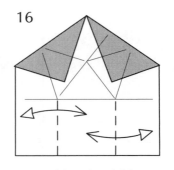

Fold and unfold.

17

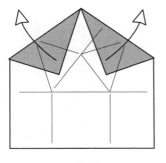

Unfold.

18

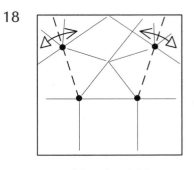

Fold and unfold.

19

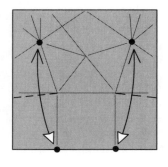

Fold and unfold each
side seperately.

20

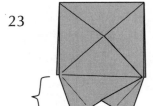

The model will become
three-dimensional.

21

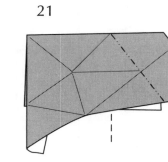

Repeat step 20
on the right.

22

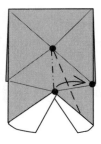

Puff out at the
upper dot.

23

Flatten at the bottom.

24

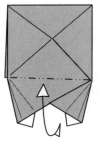

Fold and unfold.

25

Tuck inside
the pocket.

26

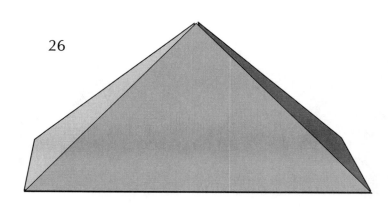

Fortress

Pyramid

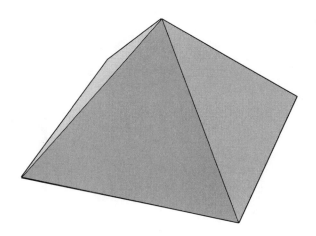

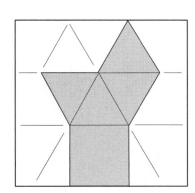

This classically proportioned pyamid is formed from a square base and four equilateral triangles and has an apex angle of 60°. The crease pattern shows a hexagon above a square. The line dividing the two shapes is formed in step 5.

1

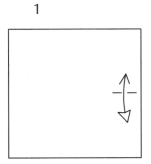

Fold and unfold on the right.

2

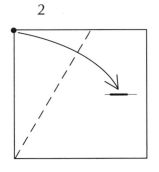

Bring the upper left corner to the center line.

3

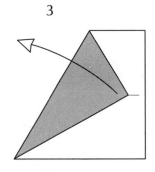

Unfold.

4

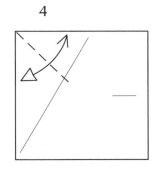

Fold and unfold.

5

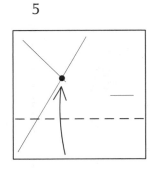

6

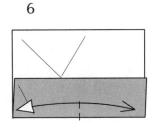

Fold and unfold.

7

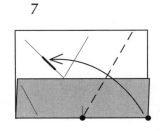

8

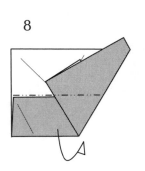

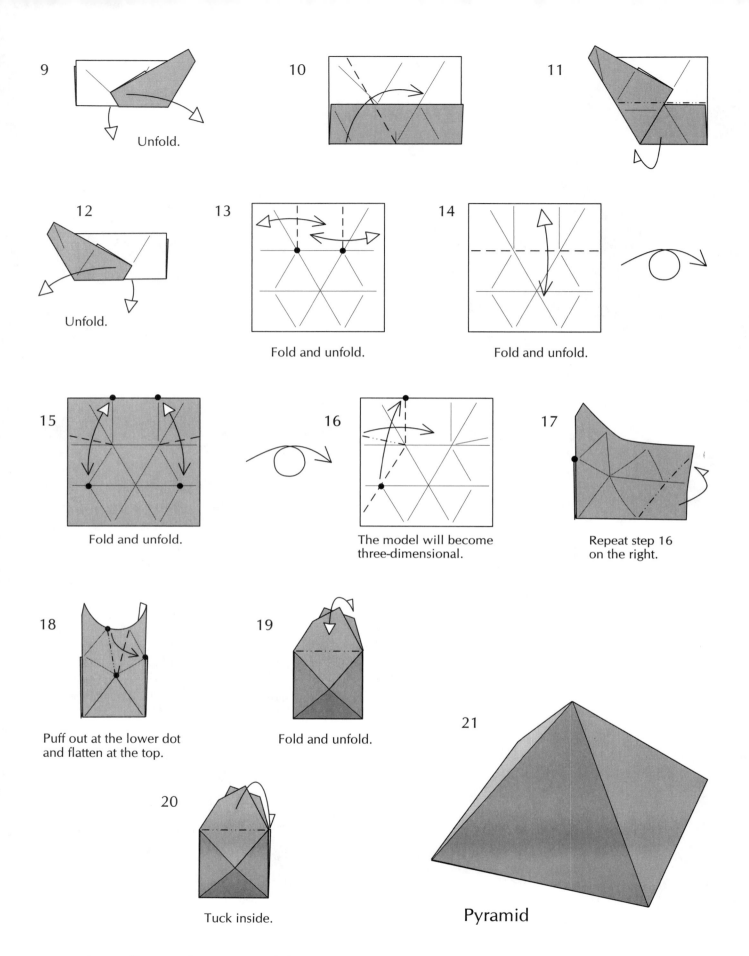

9 Unfold.

10

11

12 Unfold.

13 Fold and unfold.

14 Fold and unfold.

15 Fold and unfold.

16 The model will become three-dimensional.

17 Repeat step 16 on the right.

18 Puff out at the lower dot and flatten at the top.

19 Fold and unfold.

20 Tuck inside.

21 Pyramid

Mountain

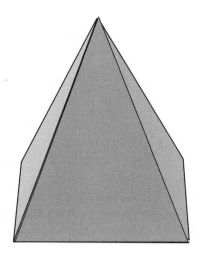

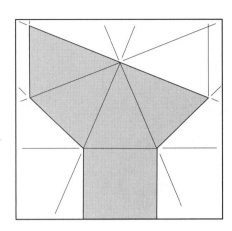

This moderately pointy pyramid is formed from a square base and four isosceles triangles, with an apex angle of 45°. The crease pattern shows a partial octagon above a square. The link between the two is formed in step 7.

1

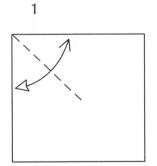

Fold and unfold.

2

Fold and unfold.

3

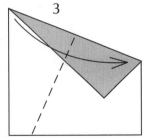

4

Unfold.

5

Fold and unfold.

6

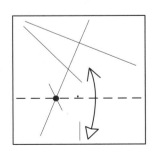

Fold and unfold, creasing at the intersection.

7

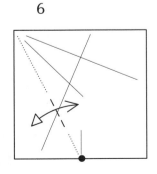

Fold and unfold.

8

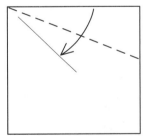

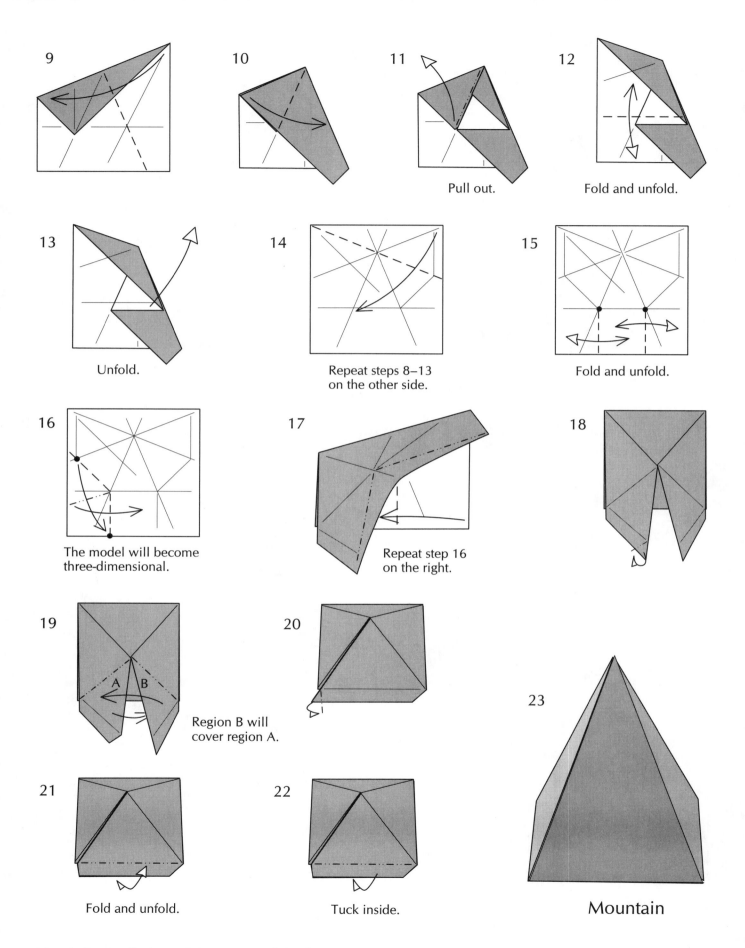

9

10

11

Pull out.

12

Fold and unfold.

13

Unfold.

14

Repeat steps 8–13
on the other side.

15

Fold and unfold.

16

The model will become
three-dimensional.

17

Repeat step 16
on the right.

18

19

Region B will
cover region A.

A B

20

21

Fold and unfold.

22

Tuck inside.

23

Mountain

Tower

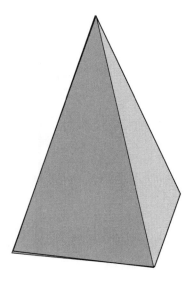

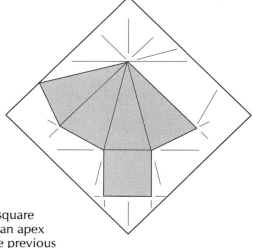

This pointy pyramid is formed from a square base and four isosceles triangles, with an apex angle of 30°. The crease patterns of the previous pyramids were symmetric when divided in half by a book fold. This and the remaining pyramids are symmetric about the diagonal.

1

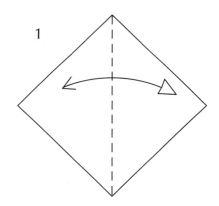

Fold and unfold creasing lightly.

2

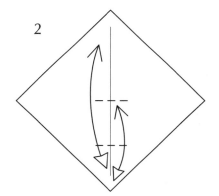

Fold and unfold creasing lightly.

3

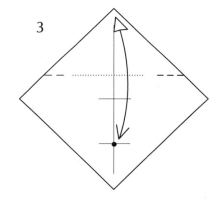

Fold and unfold creasing at the ends.

4

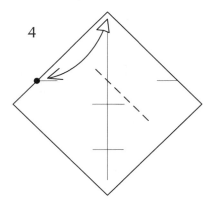

Fold and unfold, creasing at the center.

5

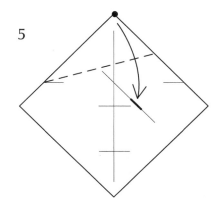

6

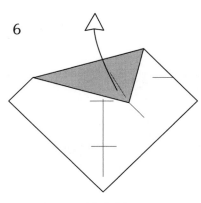

Unfold.

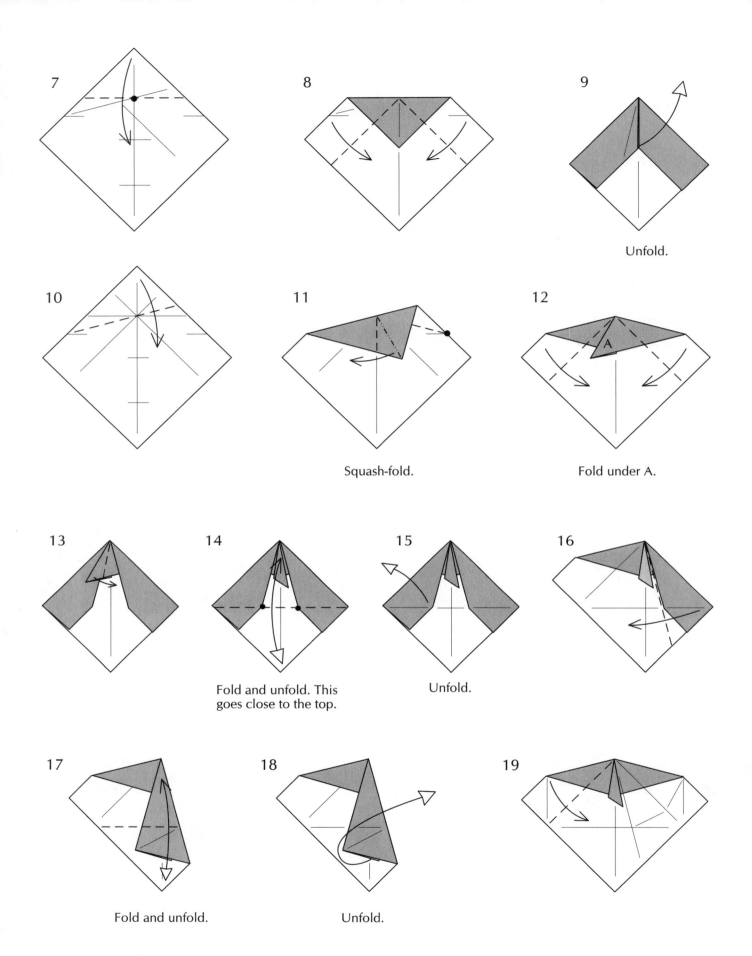

7

8

9

Unfold.

10

11

Squash-fold.

12

Fold under A.

13

14

Fold and unfold. This goes close to the top.

15

Unfold.

16

17

Fold and unfold.

18

Unfold.

19

20

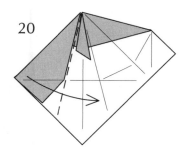

Repeat steps 16–18 on the left.

21

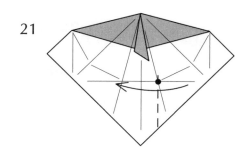

22

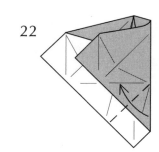

23

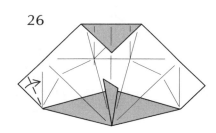

Unfold.

24

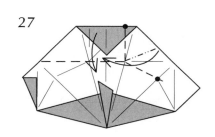

Fold and unfold.

25

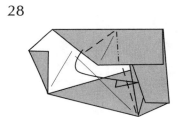

Rotate.

26

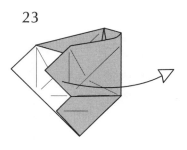

27

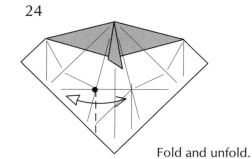

Bring the dots together as the
model becomes three-dimensional.

28

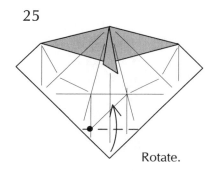

29

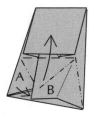

Tuck A inside B.

30

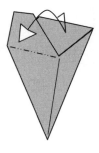

Fold and
unfold the tab.

31

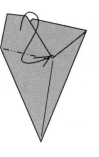

Tuck inside
and rotate.

32

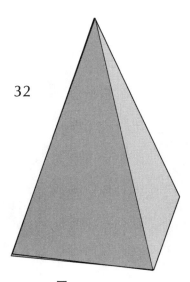

Tower

Monument

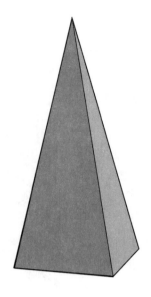

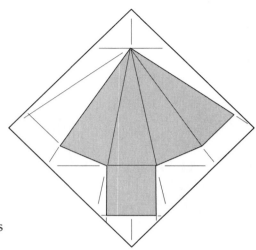

This even pointier pyramid is formed from a square base and four isosceles triangles, with an apex angle of 22.5°.

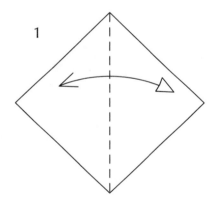

1

Fold and unfold.

2

Fold and unfold creasing lightly.

3

Fold and unfold creasing lightly.

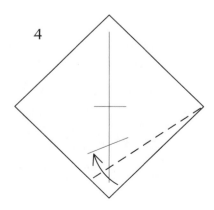

4

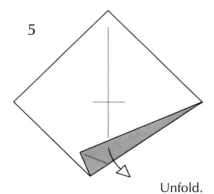

5

Unfold.

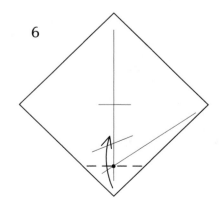

6

7

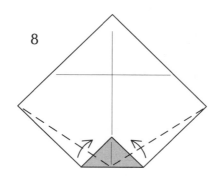

Fold and unfold.

8

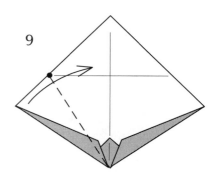

9

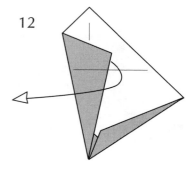

10

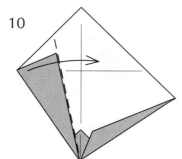

11

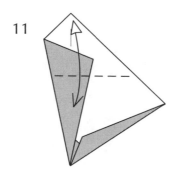

Fold and unfold.

12

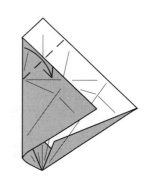

Unfold.

13

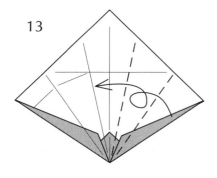

Repeat steps 9–12 on the right.

14

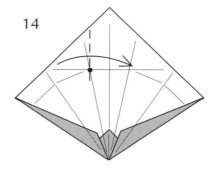

Crease at the top.

15

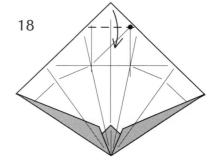

16

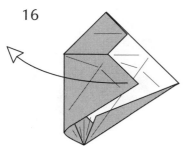

Unfold.

17

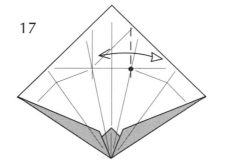

Fold and unfold.

18

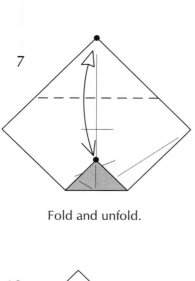

19

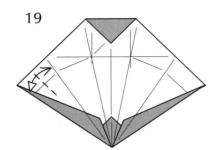

Fold and unfold.

20

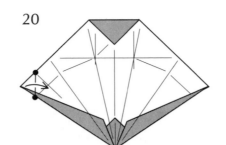

21

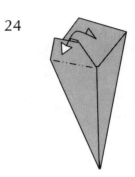

Bring the pair of dots together as the
model becomes three-dimensional.

22

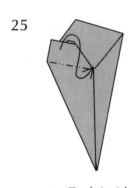

23

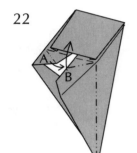

Tuck A inside B.

24

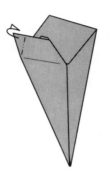

Fold and unfold the tab.

25

Tuck inside
and rotate.

26

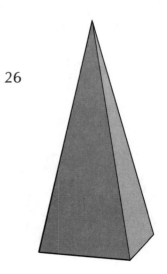

Monument

Needle

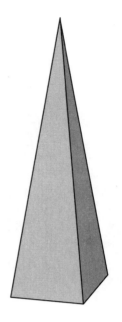

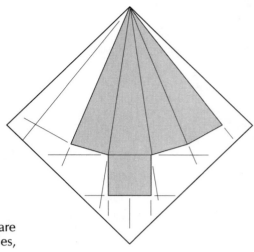

This exceptionally pointy pyramid is formed from a square base and four isosceles triangles, with an apex angle of 15°.

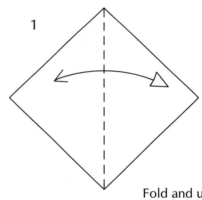

1

Fold and unfold creasing lightly.

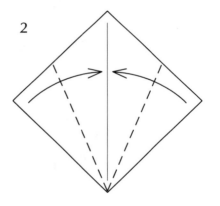

2

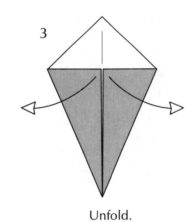

3

Unfold.

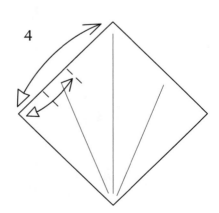

4

Fold and unfold.

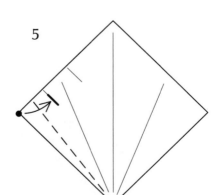

5

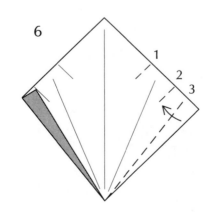

6

Repeat steps 4–5 on the right.

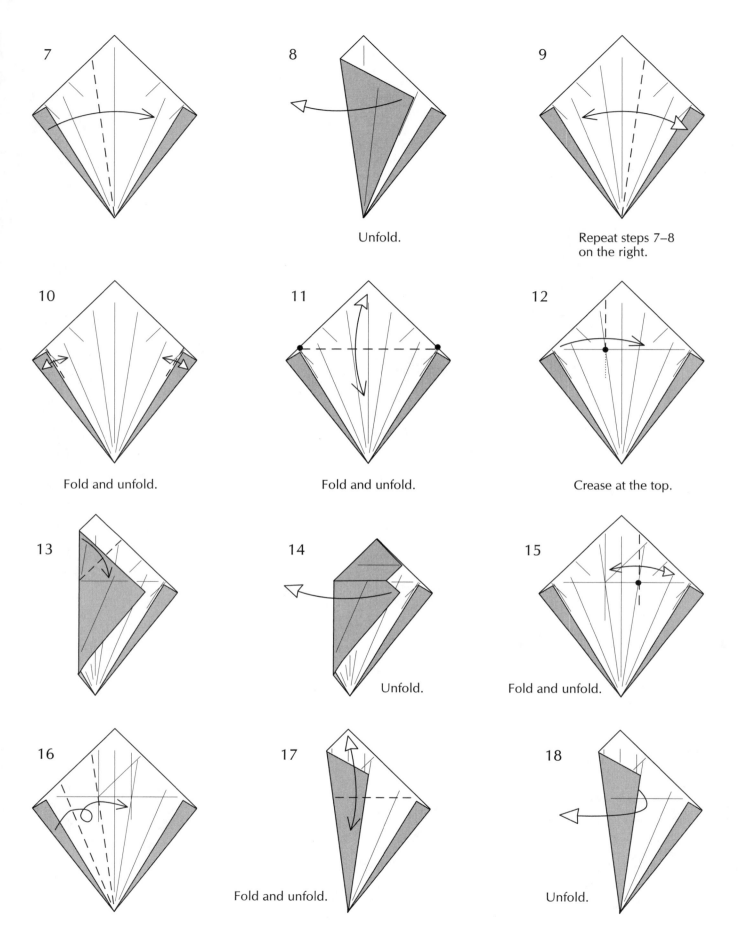

7

8

Unfold.

9

Repeat steps 7–8
on the right.

10

Fold and unfold.

11

Fold and unfold.

12

Crease at the top.

13

14

Unfold.

15

Fold and unfold.

16

17

Fold and unfold.

18

Unfold.

19

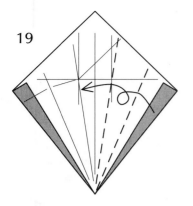

Repeat steps 16–18
on the right.

20

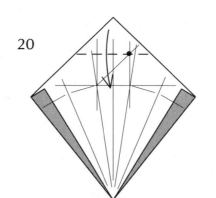

21

22

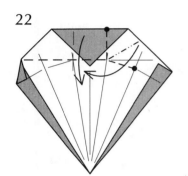

Bring the dots together as the
model becomes three-dimensional.

23

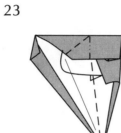

24

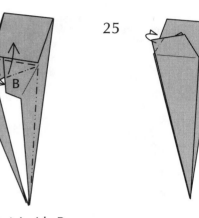

Tuck A inside B.

25

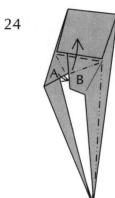

26

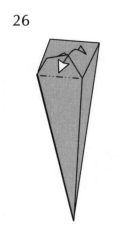

Fold and unfold the tab.

27

Tuck inside
and rotate.

28

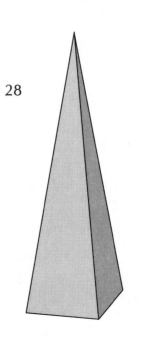

Needle

Deltahedra

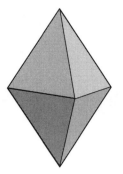

Tetrahedron
page 29

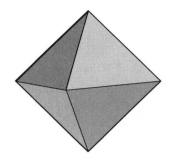

Triangular Dipyramid
page 31

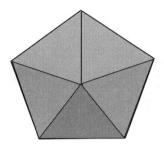

Octahedron
page 33

Pentagonal Dipyramid
page 36

Dodecadeltahedron
page 38

Triaugmented Triangular Prism
page 41

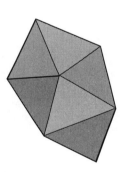

Gyroelongated Square Dipyramid
page 44

Icosahedron
page 47

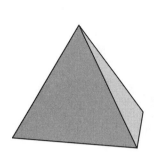

Deltahedra are polyhedra whose sides are equilateral triangles. There are eight convex deltahedra (convex means any line connecting the vertices are on or inside the solid). Three—the tetrahedron, octahedron, and icosahedron—are Platonic solids. The remaining five are irregular shapes that each have interesting symmetries and other properties, and each has several names.

The designs for all of these solids have odd symmetry, that is, the crease pattern is the same when rotated 180° (with the exception of the octahedron). One interesting result of this is that, because the deltahedra all have an even number of faces, the center of the paper in the fold pattern lies at the midpoint of an edge of the folded solid. This results in a very efficient use of the paper.

Deltahedra	Number of Sides
Tetrahedron	4
Triangular Dipyramid	6
Octahedron	8
Pentagonal Dipyramid	10
Dodecadeltahedron	12
Triaugmented Triangular Prism	14
Gyroelongated Square Dipyramid	16
Icosahedron	20

Tetrahedron

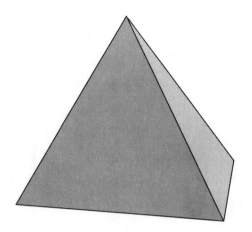

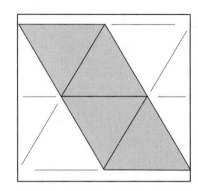

The tetrahedron, a Platonic solid composed of
four triangles, is one of the simplest polyhedra.
The crease pattern shows it is constructed with
a band of four triangles, a theme that will
continue with several other deltahedra.

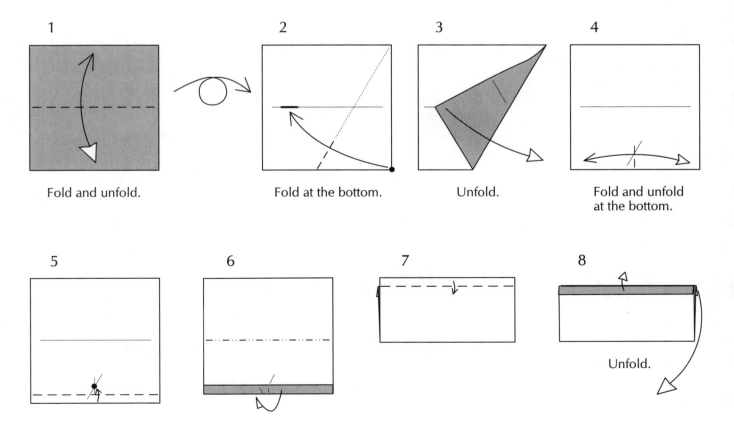

1

Fold and unfold.

2

Fold at the bottom.

3

Unfold.

4

Fold and unfold
at the bottom.

5

6

7

8

Unfold.

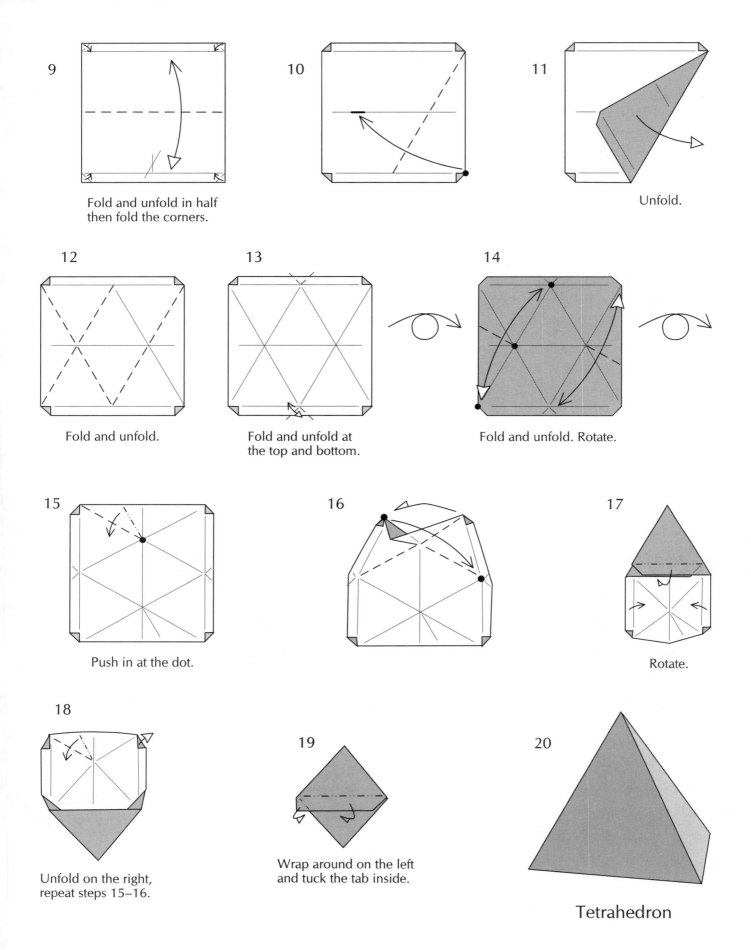

9

Fold and unfold in half
then fold the corners.

10

11

Unfold.

12

Fold and unfold.

13

Fold and unfold at
the top and bottom.

14

Fold and unfold. Rotate.

15

Push in at the dot.

16

17

Rotate.

18

Unfold on the right,
repeat steps 15–16.

19

Wrap around on the left
and tuck the tab inside.

20

Tetrahedron

Triangular Dipyramid

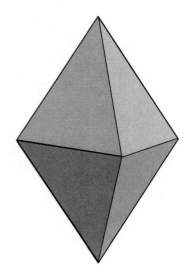

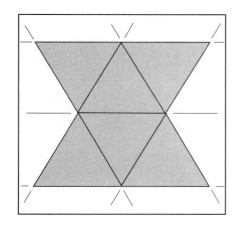

The triangular dipyramid, or hexadeltahedron, is composed of six triangular faces.

1

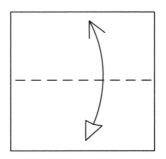

Fold and unfold.

2

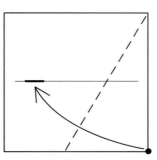

3

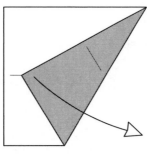

Unfold.

4

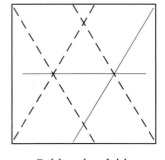

Fold and unfold three more times.

5

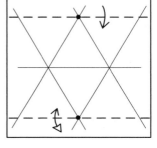

Fold and unfold at the bottom. Rotate.

6

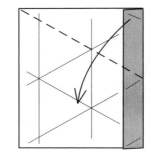

7

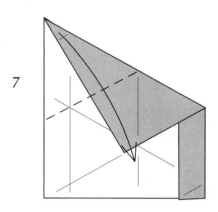

8

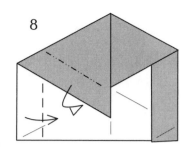

9

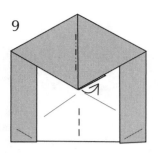

Open slightly
and rotate.

10

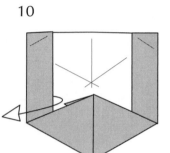

Unfold without creasing.

11

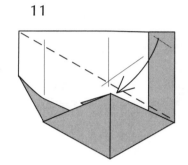

The model is three-dimensional. Fold
part way down. (Do not flatten.)

12

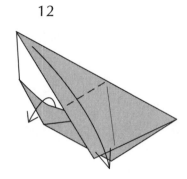

13

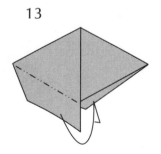

14

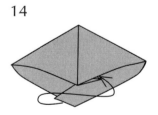

Interlock the
tabs and rotate.

15

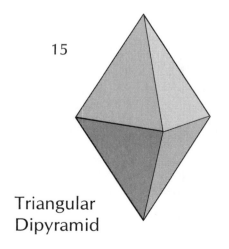

Triangular
Dipyramid

Octahedron

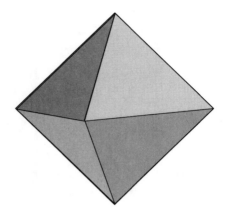

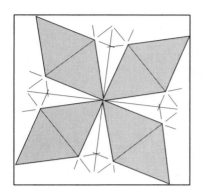

In designing the octahedron, I was searching for the easiest way to fold the most efficient one (for size) with no crease marks on the sides. This method has square symmetry; the crease pattern is the same when rotated 90°. The model closes with four thin tabs interlocking at the top, a concept called the twist lock. The thin tabs allow for efficient use of paper and have led to other designs in this collection.

1

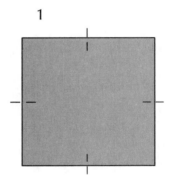

Make small marks by folding and unfolding in half.

2

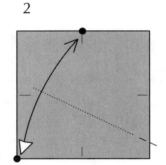

Fold and unfold on the right. Rotate.

3

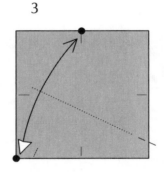

Repeat step 2 three more times.

4

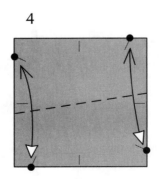

Bring the pair of dots together and unfold. Rotate.

5

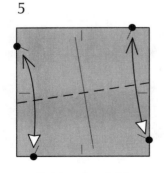

Fold and unfold.

6

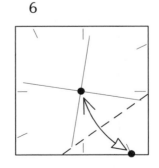

Fold and unfold. Rotate.

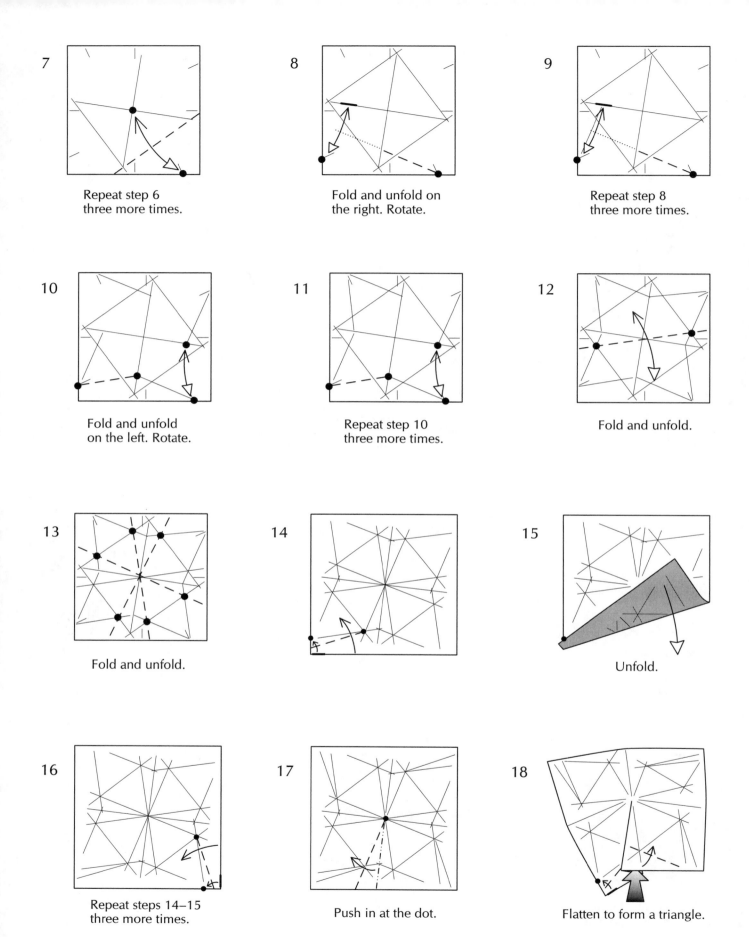

7 Repeat step 6
three more times.

8 Fold and unfold on
the right. Rotate.

9 Repeat step 8
three more times.

10 Fold and unfold
on the left. Rotate.

11 Repeat step 10
three more times.

12 Fold and unfold.

13 Fold and unfold.

14

15 Unfold.

16 Repeat steps 14–15
three more times.

17 Push in at the dot.

18 Flatten to form a triangle.

19

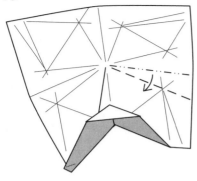

The orientation of the white triangle is not important. Repeat steps 17–18 three more times. Rotate to view the outside.

20

Flatten.

21

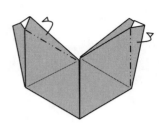

Turn over and repeat.

22

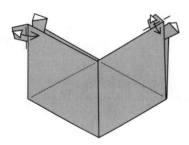

Fold and unfold.
Repeat behind.

23

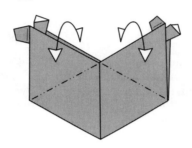

Open to fold inside and unfold.
Do not flatten. Repeat behind.

24

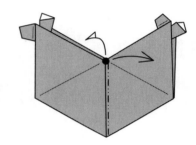

Open and flatten. Follow the dot in the next step.

25

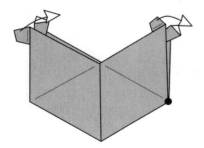

Unfold the thin flaps.
Repeat behind.

26

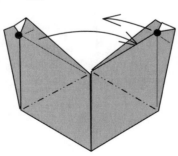

Close the model by interlocking the four tabs. These tabs spiral inward. This method is called a twist lock.

27

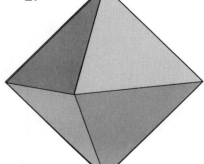

Octahedron

Pentagonal Dipyramid

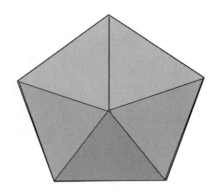

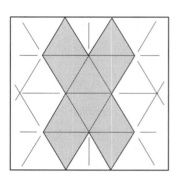

The pentagonal dipyramid, or decadeltahedron, has ten sides. It is a squat diamond, as compared to the pentagonal dipyramid in the next section, which, though it shares the same name, is more elongated.

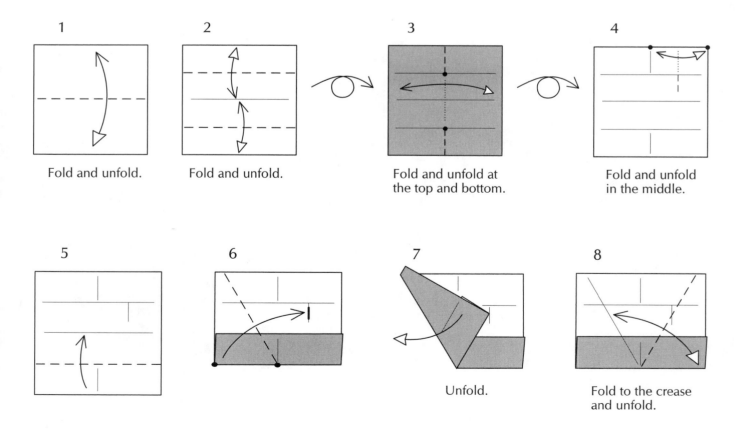

1 Fold and unfold.

2 Fold and unfold.

3 Fold and unfold at the top and bottom.

4 Fold and unfold in the middle.

5

6

7 Unfold.

8 Fold to the crease and unfold.

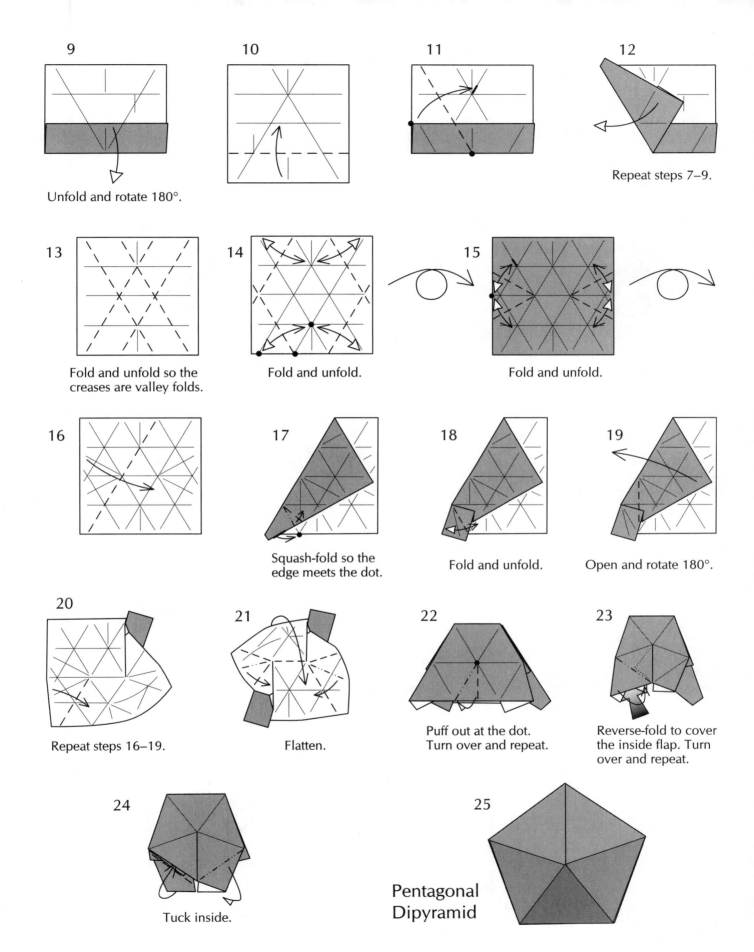

9

Unfold and rotate 180°.

10

11

12

Repeat steps 7–9.

13

Fold and unfold so the creases are valley folds.

14

Fold and unfold.

15

Fold and unfold.

16

17

Squash-fold so the edge meets the dot.

18

Fold and unfold.

19

Open and rotate 180°.

20

Repeat steps 16–19.

21

Flatten.

22

Puff out at the dot. Turn over and repeat.

23

Reverse-fold to cover the inside flap. Turn over and repeat.

24

Tuck inside.

25

Pentagonal Dipyramid

Dodecadeltahedron

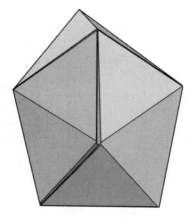

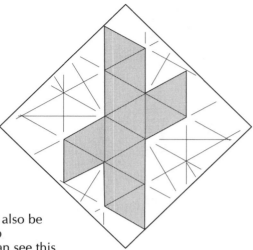

The twelve-sided dodecadeltahedron can also be called the Siamese dodecahedron or snub disphenoid. For the crease pattern, you can see this intriguing shape is constructed from a band of triangles along the diagonal, meeting the edges at the tips. Robert Lang's Reference Finder software was used to generate the folding sequence (steps 1–5) to place the key fold to develop that geometry.

1

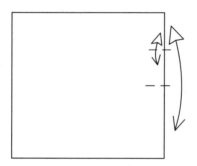

Fold and unfold on the right to find the quarter mark.

2

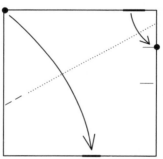

Bring the top edge to the dot on the right and the top left corner to the bottom edge. Crease on the left.

3

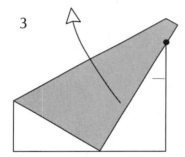

Unfold.

4

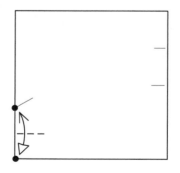

Fold and unfold on the left.

5

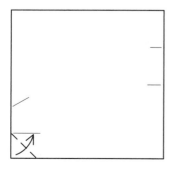

Fold to the crease and rotate.

6

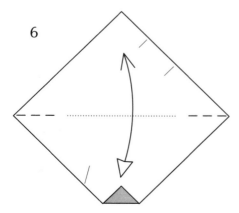

Fold and unfold on the left and right.

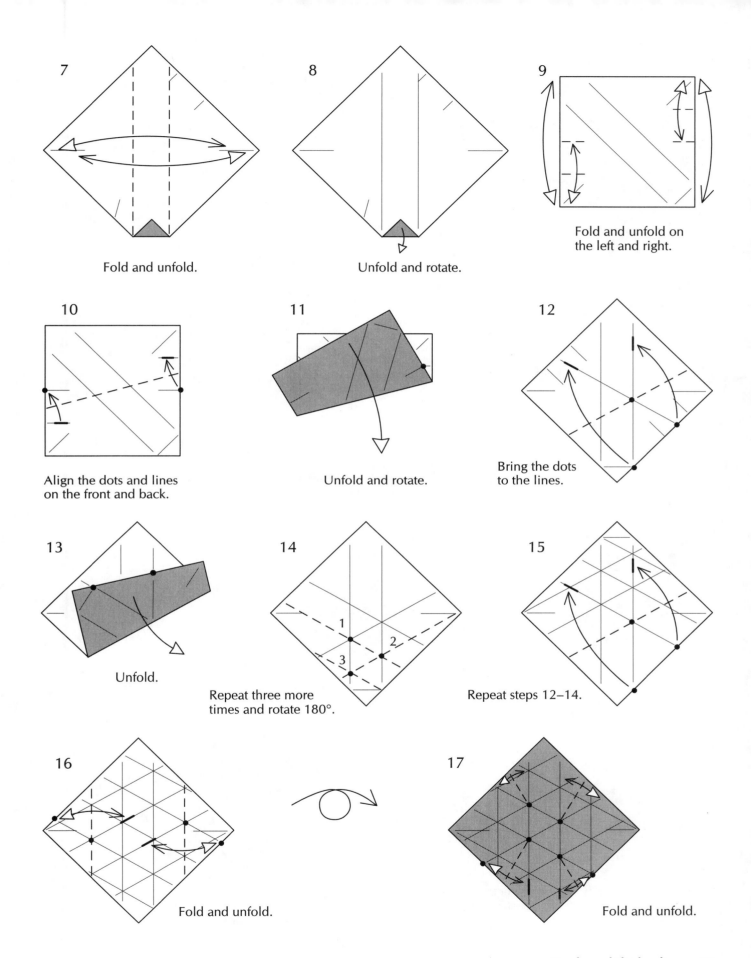

7

Fold and unfold.

8

Unfold and rotate.

9

Fold and unfold on
the left and right.

10

Align the dots and lines
on the front and back.

11

Unfold and rotate.

12

Bring the dots
to the lines.

13

Unfold.

14

Repeat three more
times and rotate 180°.

15

Repeat steps 12–14.

16

Fold and unfold.

17

Fold and unfold.

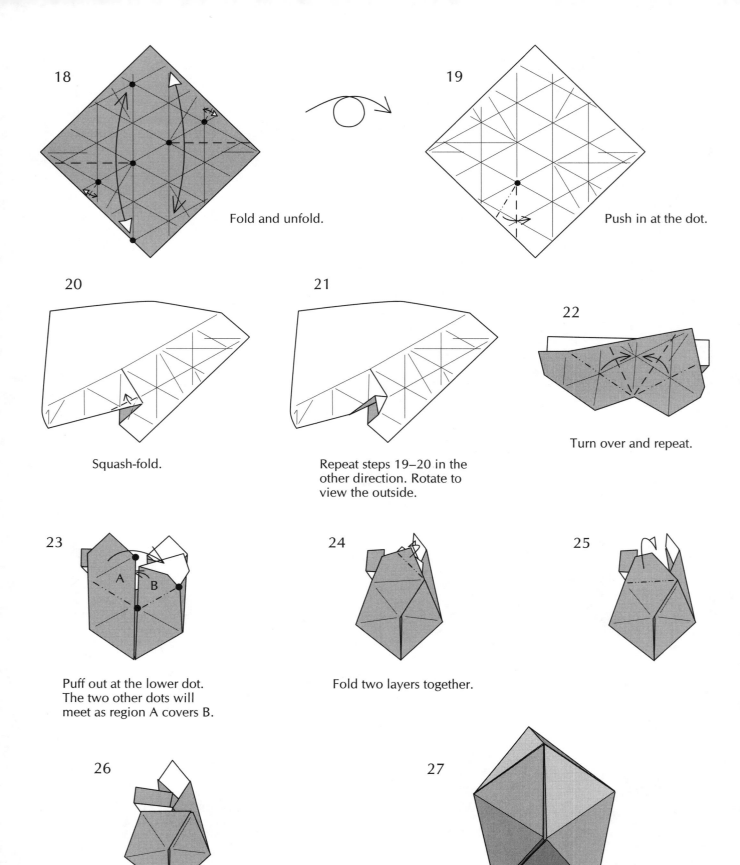

18 Fold and unfold.

19 Push in at the dot.

20 Squash-fold.

21 Repeat steps 19–20 in the other direction. Rotate to view the outside.

22 Turn over and repeat.

23 Puff out at the lower dot. The two other dots will meet as region A covers B.

24 Fold two layers together.

25

26 Turn over and repeat steps 23–25.

27 Dodecadeltahedron

Triaugmented Triangular Prism

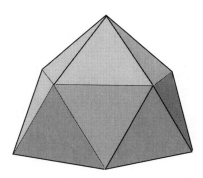

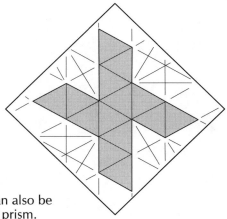

The fourteen-sided triaugmented triangular prism can also be called tetrakaidecadeltahedron or tetrakis triangular prism. The folding method is similar to the dodecadeltahedron, using a band of triangles along the diagonal. It closes with a twist lock, similar to that of the octahedron. This shape exhibits a combination of symmetries unique among the deltahedra. Robert Lang's Reference Finder software was used to generate the folding sequence (steps 1–5) to place the key fold to develop that geometry.

1

Fold and unfold on the right.

2

Fold and unfold on the bottom.

3

Fold and unfold on the left.

4

Fold and unfold on the left.

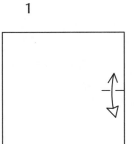

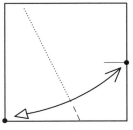

5

Fold to the crease and rotate.

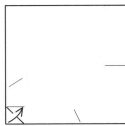

6

Fold and unfold on the left and right.

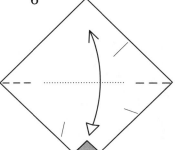

7

Fold and unfold.

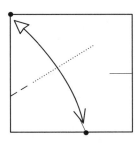

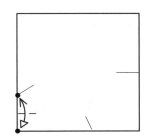

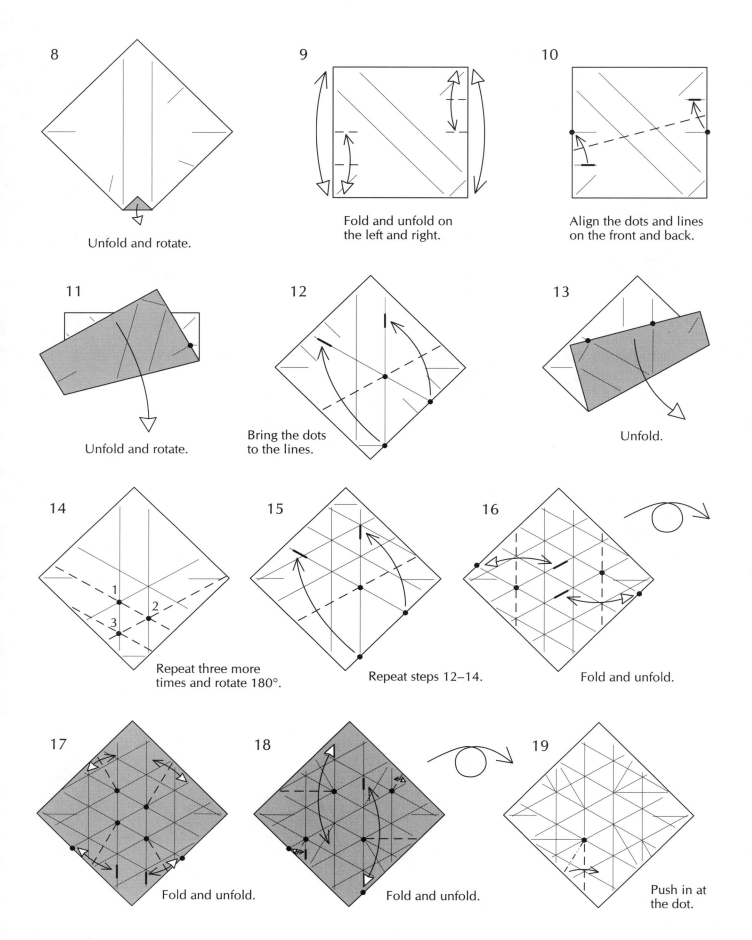

8

Unfold and rotate.

9

Fold and unfold on
the left and right.

10

Align the dots and lines
on the front and back.

11

Unfold and rotate.

12

Bring the dots
to the lines.

13

Unfold.

14

Repeat three more
times and rotate 180°.

15

Repeat steps 12–14.

16

Fold and unfold.

17

Fold and unfold.

18

Fold and unfold.

19

Push in at
the dot.

20

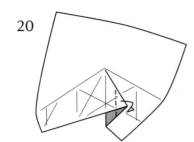

21

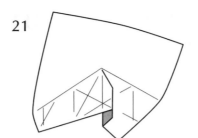

Repeat steps 19–20 on
the other side. Rotate
to view the outside.

22

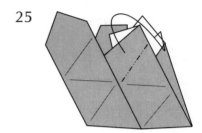

23

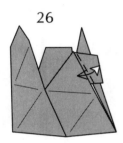

24

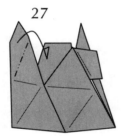

Repeat steps 22–23
going around.

25

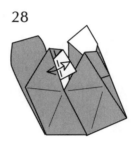

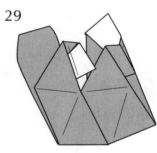

26

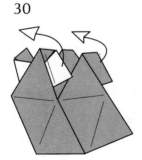

Fold and unfold.

27

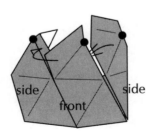

28

Fold and unfold.

29

Repeat steps 25–28
going around.

30

Unfold on four flaps.

31

side / front / side

The front and back each have four triangles.
There are two triangles on each side. Tuck
the four tabs inside, wrapping around. The
four dots (the back one not drawn) meet at
the top of the model. One method is to bring
the back, right side, and front together so the
dots meet at the top, each with tabs tucked
in, and tuck the remaining left tab last.

32

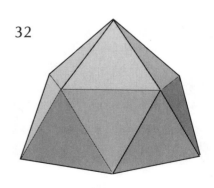

Triaugmented
Triangular Prism

Gyroelongated Square Dipyramid

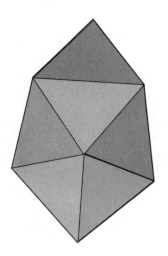

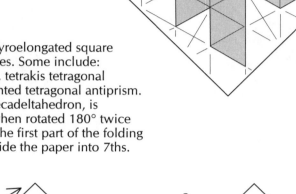

This oval sixteen-sided gyroelongated square prism goes by other names. Some include: hexakaidecadeltahedron, tetrakis tetragonal antiprism, and bi-augmented tetragonal antiprism. This shape, like the dodecadeltahedron, is symmetrical with itself when rotated 180° twice on perpendicular axes. The first part of the folding sequence (steps 1–8) divide the paper into 7ths.

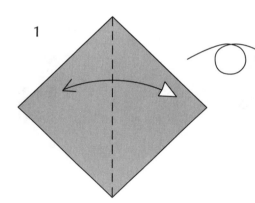

1

Fold and unfold.

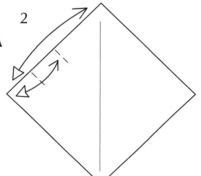

2

Fold and unfold to find the quarter mark.

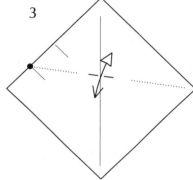

3

Fold and unfold creasing on the diagonal.

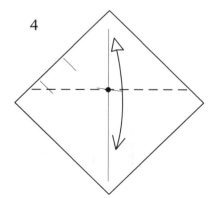

4

Fold and unfold. This divides the diagonal into 3/7 and 4/7.

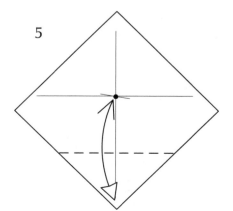

5

Fold and unfold.

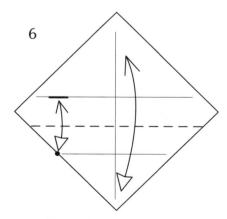

6

Fold and unfold.

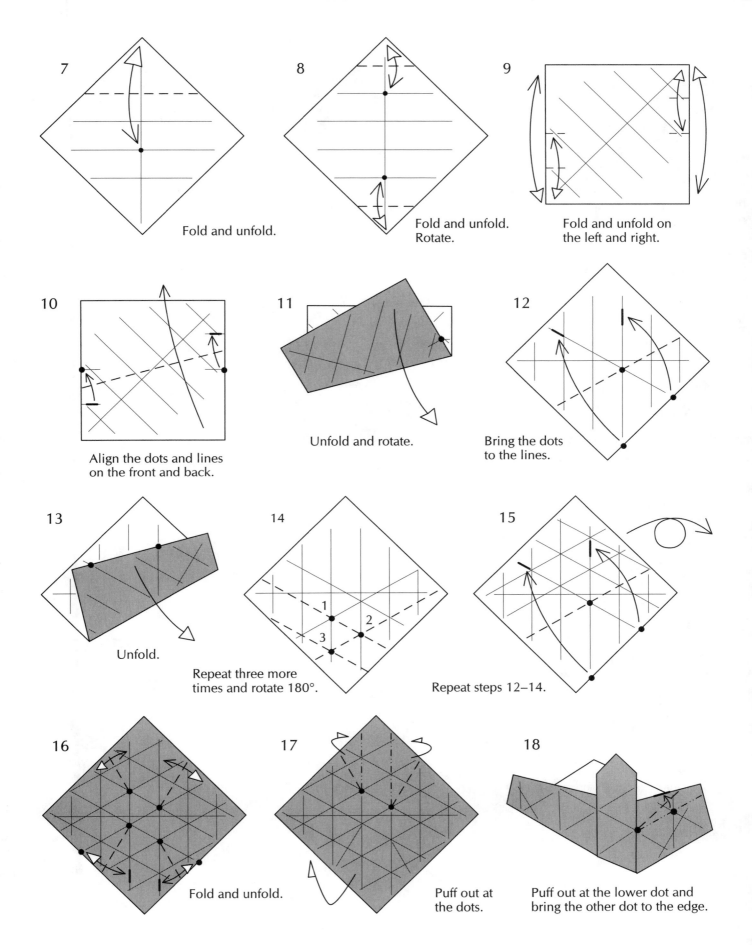

7

Fold and unfold.

8

Fold and unfold.
Rotate.

9

Fold and unfold on
the left and right.

10

Align the dots and lines
on the front and back.

11

Unfold and rotate.

12

Bring the dots
to the lines.

13

Unfold.

14

1
2
3

Repeat three more
times and rotate 180°.

15

Repeat steps 12–14.

16

Fold and unfold.

17

Puff out at
the dots.

18

Puff out at the lower dot and
bring the other dot to the edge.

19

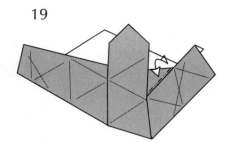

Fold and unfold
on one layer.

20

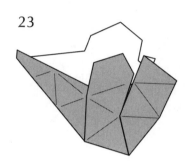

Fold on a hidden layer to
bring the dots together.

21

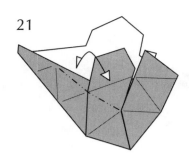

Fold and unfold.

22

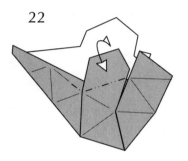

Fold and unfold.

23

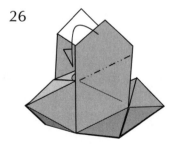

Repeat steps 17–22 behind.

24

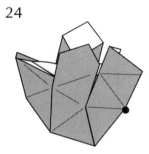

Rotate to view the dot.

25

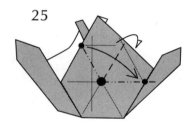

Puff out at the larger dot,
fold much of the paper
inside. Turn over and repeat.

26

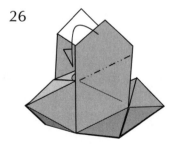

Tuck inside. Turn
over and repeat.

27

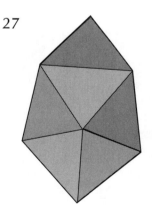

Gyroelongated
Square Dipyramid

Icosahedron

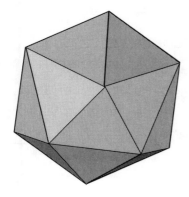

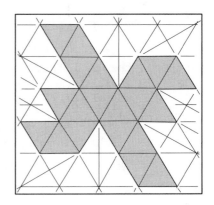

The icosahedron, with its twenty sides, concludes this section of deltahedra. The folding design for this icosahedron uses the paper efficiently, is not so difficult to fold, holds well, and has no stray creases on the faces.

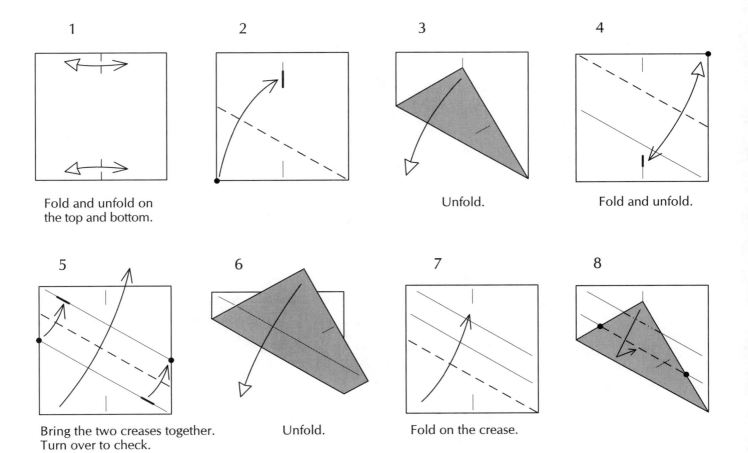

1

Fold and unfold on the top and bottom.

2

3

Unfold.

4

Fold and unfold.

5

Bring the two creases together. Turn over to check.

6

Unfold.

7

Fold on the crease.

8

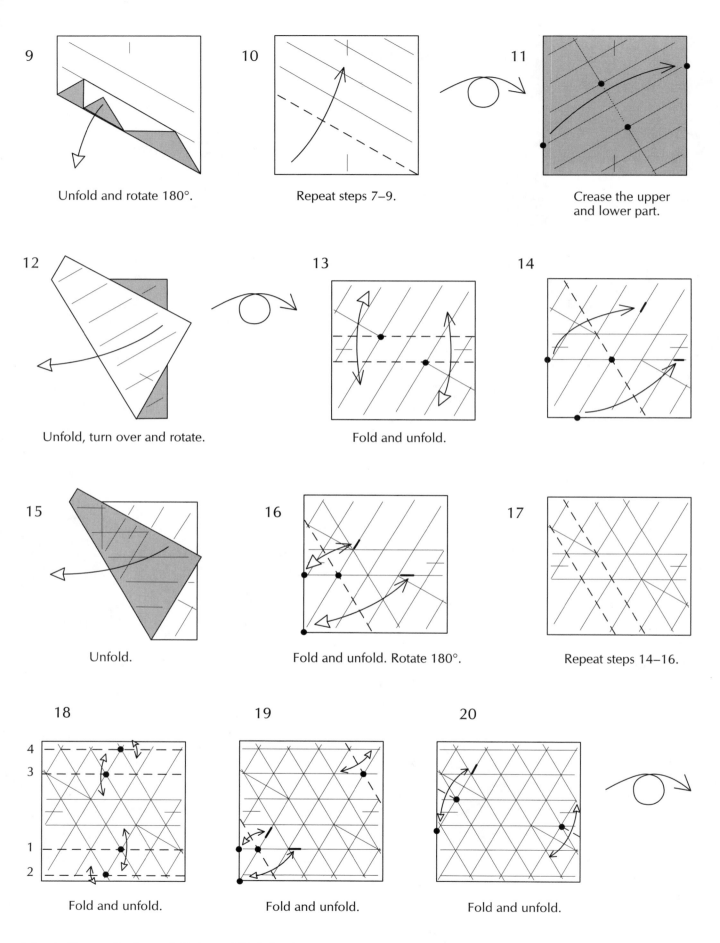

9
Unfold and rotate 180°.

10
Repeat steps 7–9.

11
Crease the upper and lower part.

12
Unfold, turn over and rotate.

13
Fold and unfold.

14

15
Unfold.

16
Fold and unfold. Rotate 180°.

17
Repeat steps 14–16.

18
Fold and unfold.

19
Fold and unfold.

20
Fold and unfold.

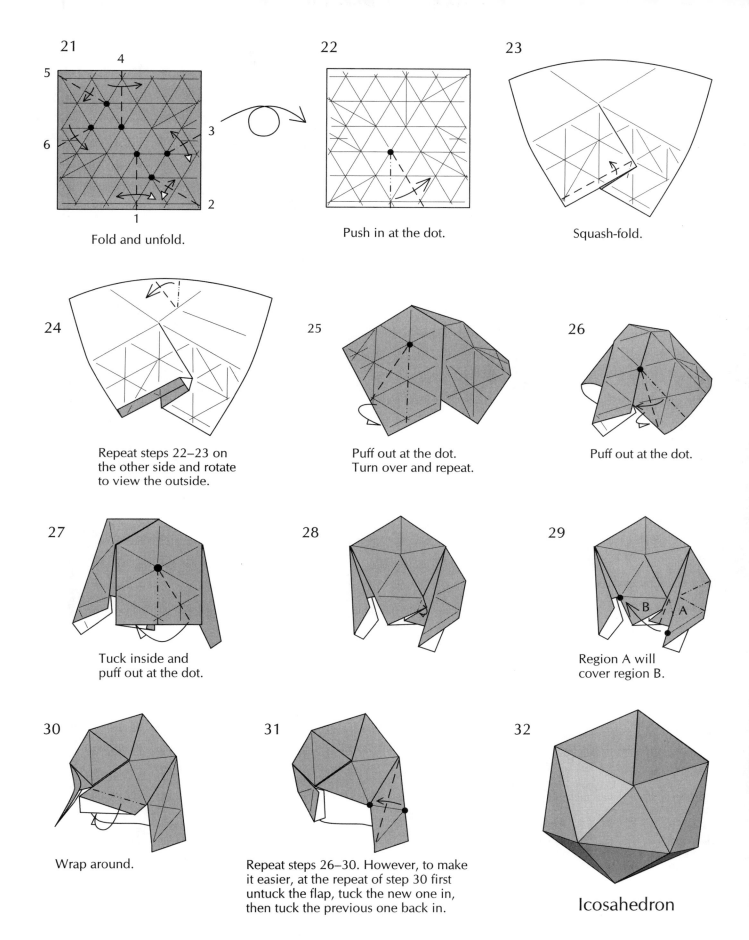

21

Fold and unfold.

22

Push in at the dot.

23

Squash-fold.

24

Repeat steps 22–23 on the other side and rotate to view the outside.

25

Puff out at the dot. Turn over and repeat.

26

Puff out at the dot.

27

Tuck inside and puff out at the dot.

28

29

Region A will cover region B.

30

Wrap around.

31

Repeat steps 26–30. However, to make it easier, at the repeat of step 30 first untuck the flap, tuck the new one in, then tuck the previous one back in.

32

Icosahedron

Diamonds

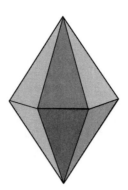

**Hexagonal
Dipyramid**
page 56

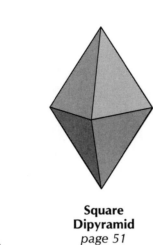

**Square
Dipyramid**
page 51

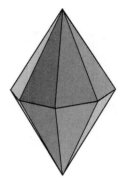

**Heptagonal
Dipyramid**
page 59

**Triangular
Dipyramid**
page 31

**Pentagonal
Dipyramid**
page 54

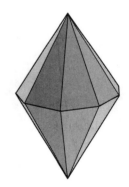

**Octagonal
Dipyramid**
page 62

This collection of diamonds range over a series of crystalline shapes of different order symmetries. For each dipyramid, the sum of the angles meeting at the top is 180°. The faces are all isosceles triangles, except for the triangular dipyramid whose faces are equilateral triangles. The triangular dipyramid is found in the deltahedra section. The crease patterns for the diamonds all have even/odd symmetry.

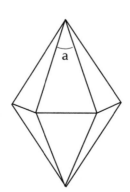

Diamond	Angle a
Triangular	60°
Square	45°
Pentagonal	36°
Hexagonal	30°
Heptagonal	25.7°
Octagonal	22.5°

Square Dipyramid

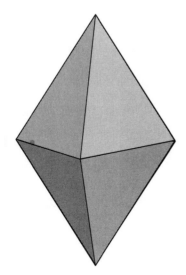

The angles of each of the eight triangles are 45°, 67.5°, and 67.5°.

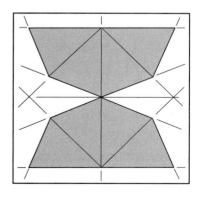

1

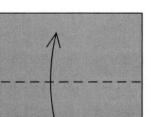

Fold and unfold.

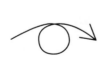

2

Fold and unfold along opposite corners.

3

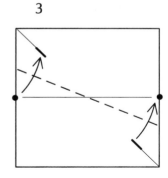

Fold to the landmarks and turn over to check on the back.

4

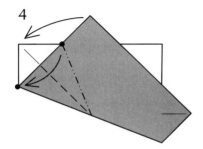

Turn over and repeat.

5

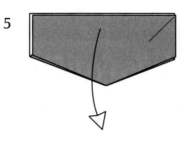

Unfold.

6

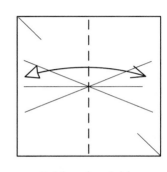

Fold and unfold.

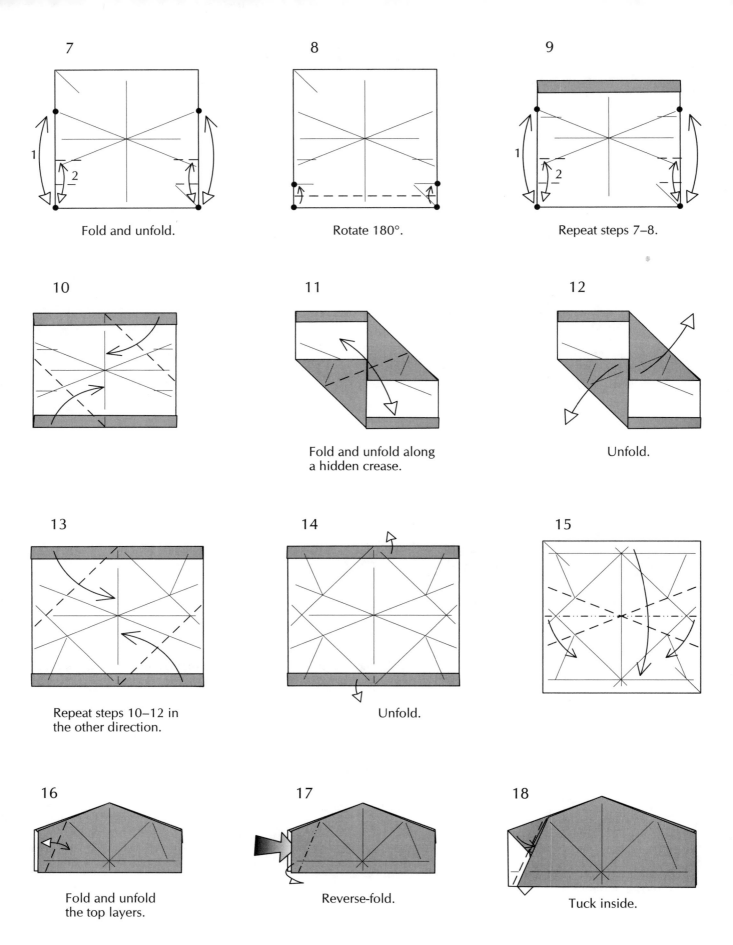

7

Fold and unfold.

8

Rotate 180°.

9

Repeat steps 7–8.

10

11

Fold and unfold along
a hidden crease.

12

Unfold.

13

Repeat steps 10–12 in
the other direction.

14

Unfold.

15

16

Fold and unfold
the top layers.

17

Reverse-fold.

18

Tuck inside.

19

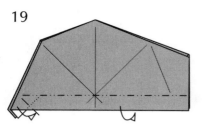

Reverse-fold on the left.

20

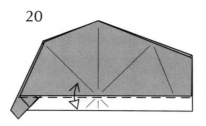

Fold and unfold.

21

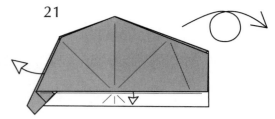

Unfold back to step 16.

22

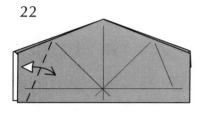

Repeat steps16–20.

23

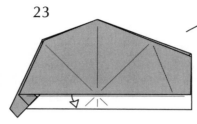

Unfold.

24

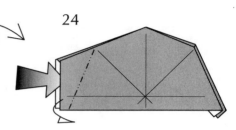

Refold steps17–18.

25

Lift up at the dot and
reverse-fold on the left.
Turn over and repeat.

26

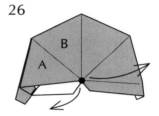

Open and bring
the dot to the right.

27

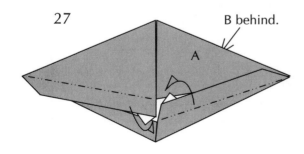

Interlock the tabs.

28

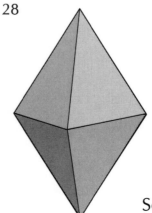

Square Dipyramid

Pentagonal Dipyramid

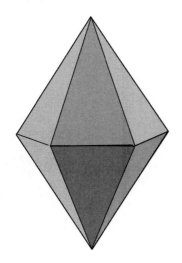

The angles of each of the ten triangles are 36°, 72°, and 72°. The crease pattern shows the faces arranged into two half decagons. The folds which establish the pentagonal geometry are made in step 3. This landmark was located using Robert Lang's Reference Finder software.

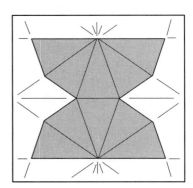

1

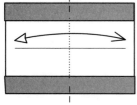

Fold and unfold.

2

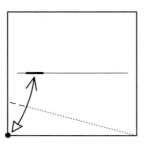

Fold and unfold the corner to the center line, creasing on the left.

3

Rotate 180°.

4

Repeat steps 2–3.

5

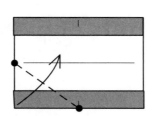

Fold and unfold at the top and bottom.

6

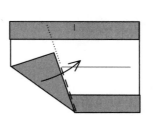

7

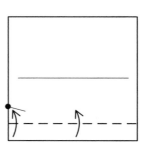

8

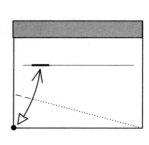

Fold and unfold.

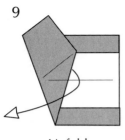

9

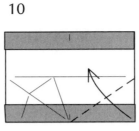

10

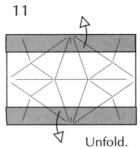

11

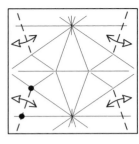

12

Unfold.

Repeat steps 6–9 on the three other corners.

Unfold.

Fold and unfold.

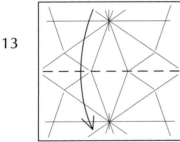

13

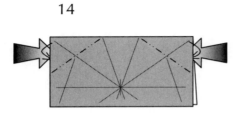

14

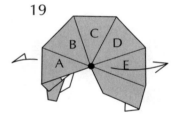

15

Reverse-fold.

Lift up the top layer to view the inside.

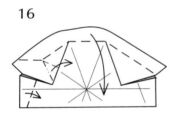

16

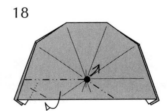

17

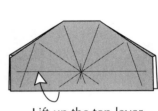

18

19

View of the inside. Fold the inside layers together.

Note how the corner is locked at the dot. Turn over and repeat steps 15–16.

Lift up at the dot and reverse-fold on the left. Turn over and repeat.

Rotate the dot to the right.

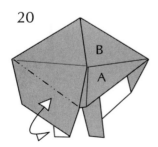

20

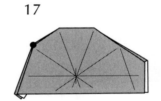

21

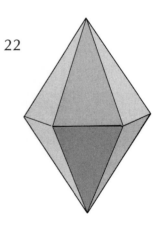

22

Fold and unfold several layers. Turn over and repeat.

Tuck and interlock the tabs.

Pentagonal Dipyramid

Hexagonal Dipyramid

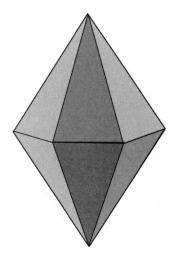

The angles of each of the twelve triangles are 30°, 75°, and 75°.

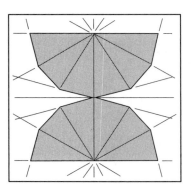

1

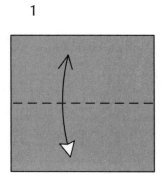

Fold and unfold.

2

Fold and unfold to make quarter marks.

3

Align the dots and lines on the front and back.

4

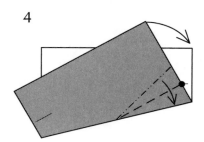

Turn over and repeat.

5

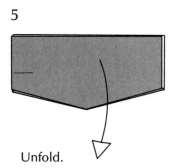

Unfold.

6

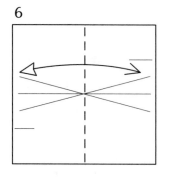

Fold and unfold.

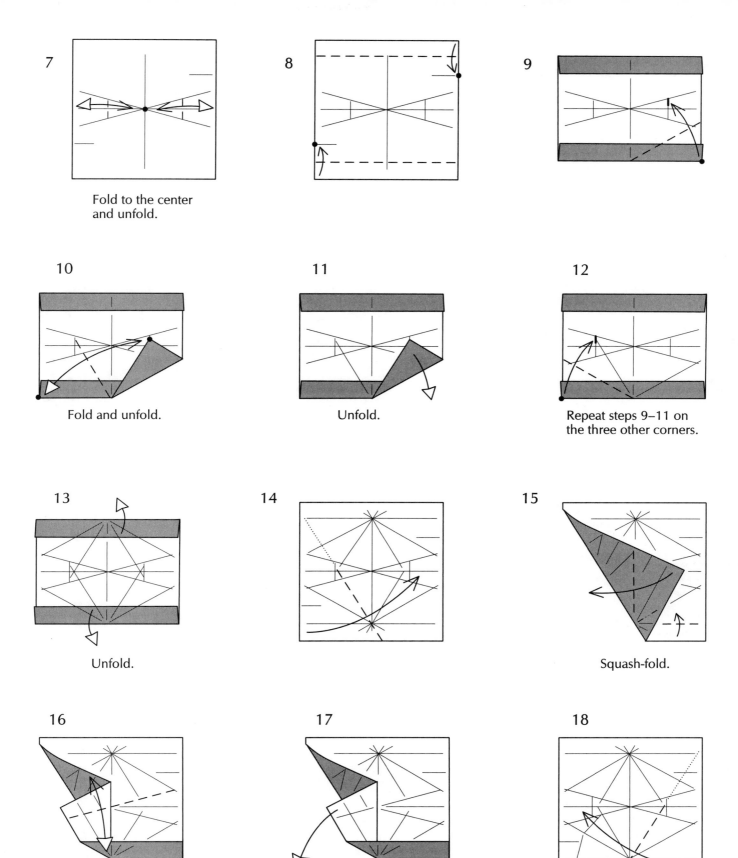

7 Fold to the center and unfold.

8

9

10 Fold and unfold.

11 Unfold.

12 Repeat steps 9–11 on the three other corners.

13 Unfold.

14

15 Squash-fold.

16 Fold and unfold.

17 Unfold.

18 Repeat steps 14–17 on the three other corners.

19

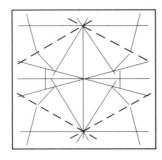

Fold and unfold.

20

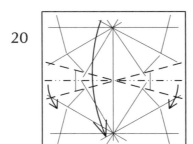

21

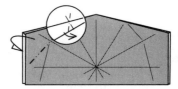

Inside view. Fold the
inside layers together.
Turn over and repeat.

22

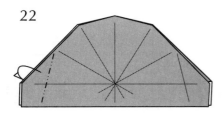

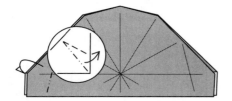

Inside view. Fold the
inside layers together.
Turn over and repeat.

23

Fold the edge to the dot.
Turn over and repeat.

24

Reverse-fold
on the left.

25

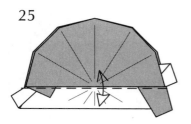

Fold and unfold.

26

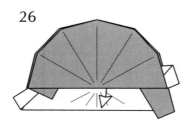

Unfold.

27

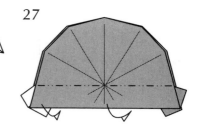

Repeat steps 24–26.

28

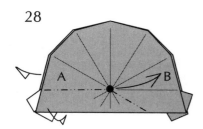

Lift up at the dot, reverse-fold
on the left, and bring the dot to
the right. Turn over and repeat.

29

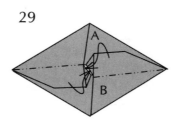

Tuck and interlock the tabs.

30

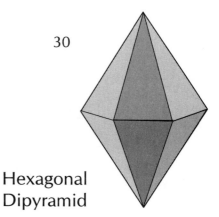

Hexagonal
Dipyramid

Heptagonal Dipyramid

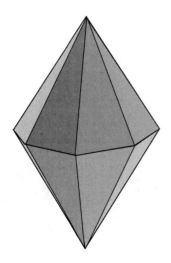

The angles of each of the fourteen triangles are 25.7°, 77°, and 77°. The crease pattern shows the faces arranged into two half 14gons. The folds which establish the geometry are made in steps 1–8, following a folding sequence determined using Robert Lang's Reference Finder software.

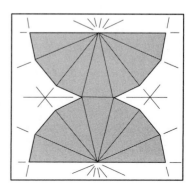

1

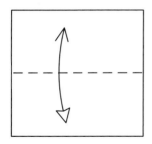

Fold and unfold.

2

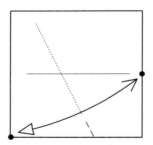

Fold and unfold, creasing at the bottom.

3

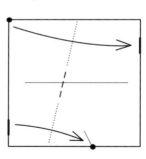

Bring the top left corner to the right edge and the left edge to the bottom dot. Only crease in the center.

4

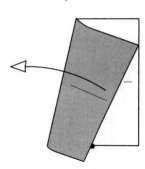

Unfold.

5

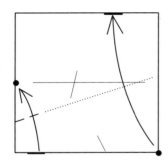

Bring the bottom right corner to the top edge and the bottom edge to the left center. Only crease on the left.

6

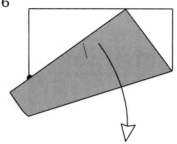

Unfold. Rotate 180°.

7

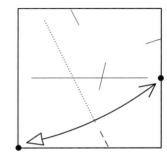

Repeat steps 2–6.

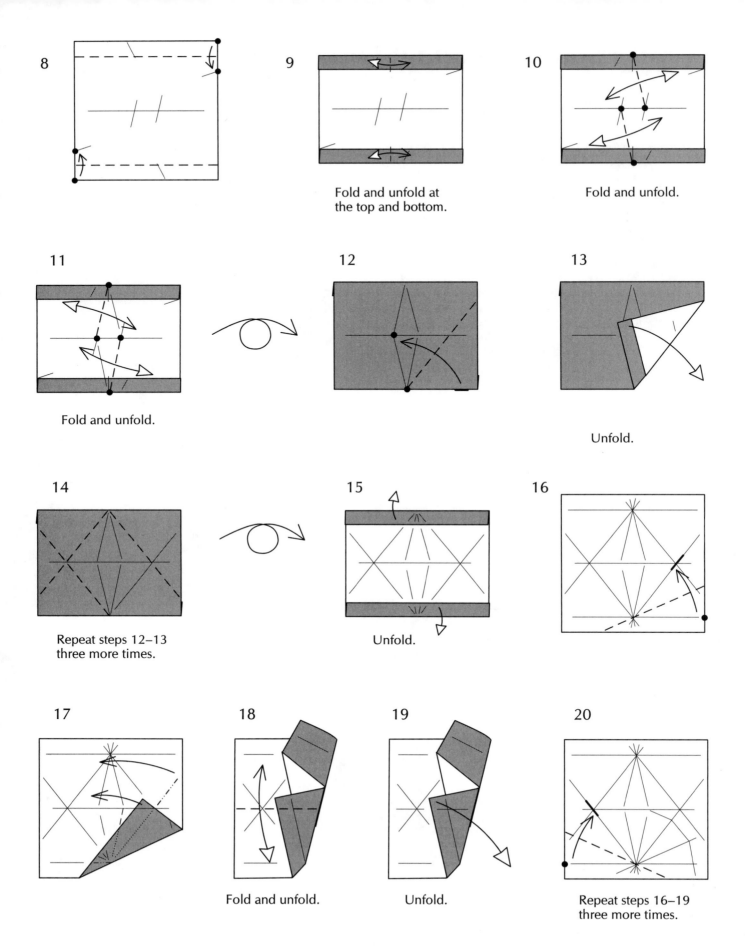

8

9

Fold and unfold at
the top and bottom.

10

Fold and unfold.

11

Fold and unfold.

12

13

Unfold.

14

Repeat steps 12–13
three more times.

15

Unfold.

16

17

18

Fold and unfold.

19

Unfold.

20

Repeat steps 16–19
three more times.

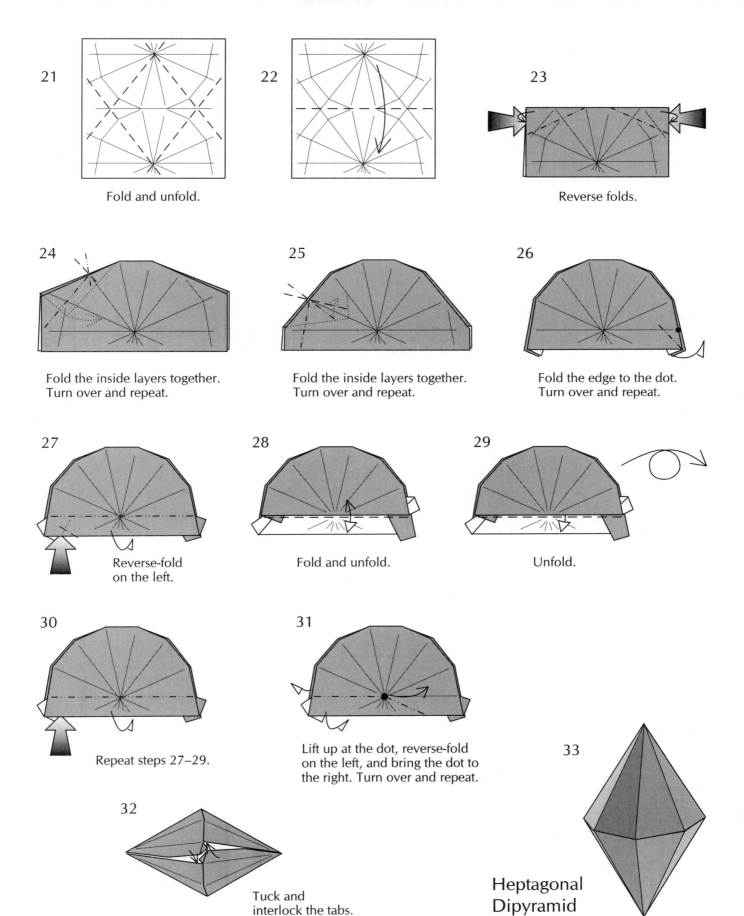

21

Fold and unfold.

22

23

Reverse folds.

24

Fold the inside layers together.
Turn over and repeat.

25

Fold the inside layers together.
Turn over and repeat.

26

Fold the edge to the dot.
Turn over and repeat.

27

Reverse-fold
on the left.

28

Fold and unfold.

29

Unfold.

30

Repeat steps 27–29.

31

Lift up at the dot, reverse-fold
on the left, and bring the dot to
the right. Turn over and repeat.

32

Tuck and
interlock the tabs.

33

Heptagonal
Dipyramid

Octagonal Dipyramid

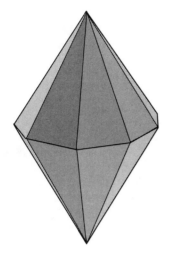

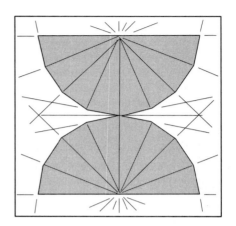

The angles of each of the
sixteen triangles are 22.5°,
78.75°, and 78.75°.

1

Fold and unfold.

2

Fold and unfold.

3

Fold the edge to the center and
unfold, creasing on the left.

4

Fold and unfold
in the center.

5

Rotate 180°.

6

Repeat steps 3–5.

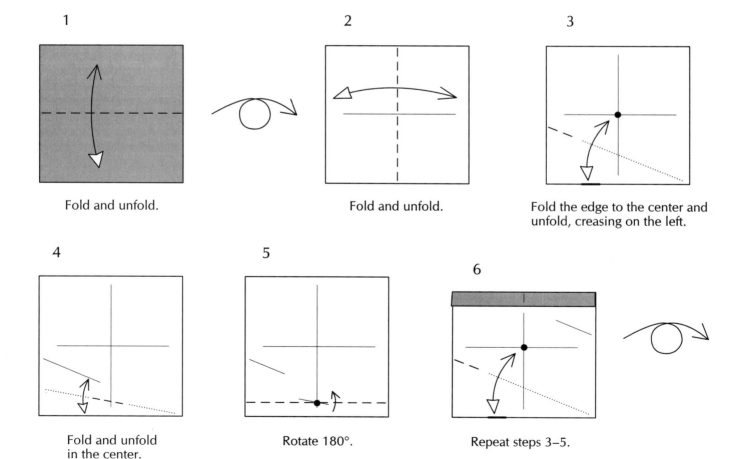

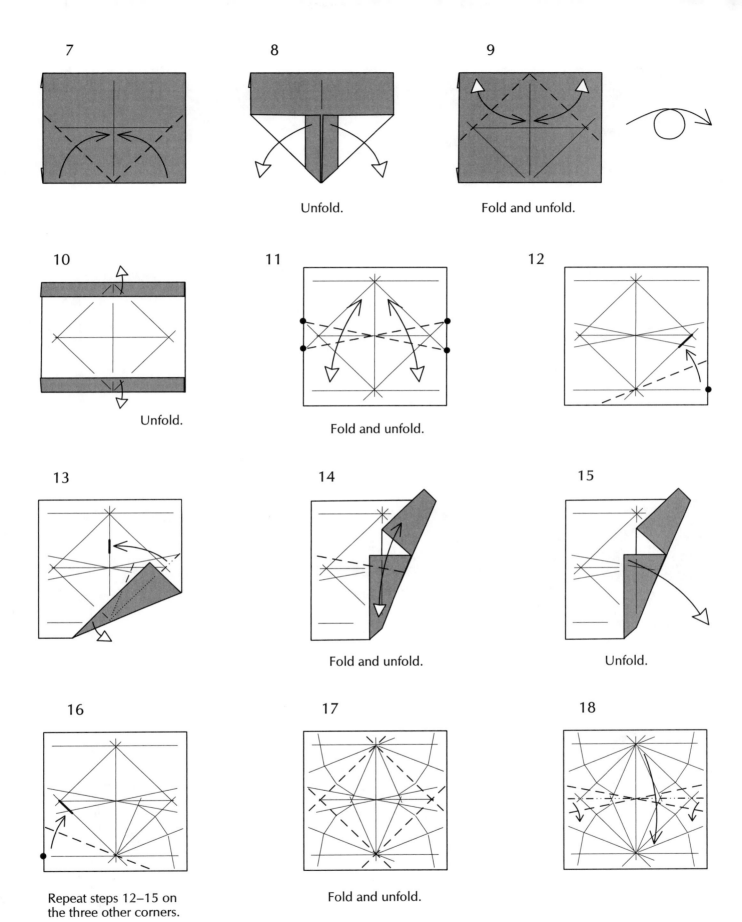

7

8

Unfold.

9

Fold and unfold.

10

Unfold.

11

Fold and unfold.

12

13

14

Fold and unfold.

15

Unfold.

16

Repeat steps 12–15 on
the three other corners.

17

Fold and unfold.

18

19

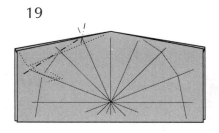

Fold the inside layers together.

20

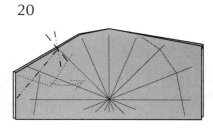

Fold the inside layers together.

21

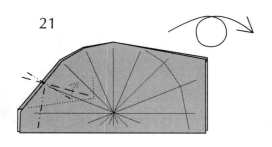

Fold the inside layers together.

22

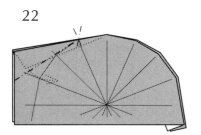

Repeat steps 19–21.

23

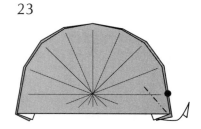

Fold the edge to the dot.
Turn over and repeat.

24

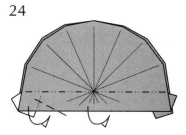

Reverse-fold on the left.

25

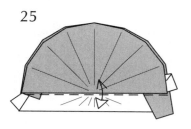

Fold and unfold.

26

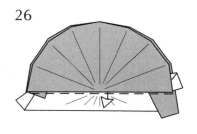

Unfold.

27

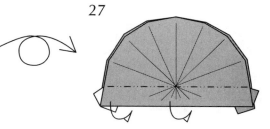

Repeat steps 24–26.

28

Lift up at the dot, reverse-fold
on the left, and bring the dot to
the right. Turn over and repeat.

29

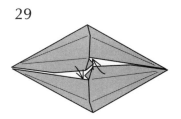

Tuck and interlock the tabs.

30

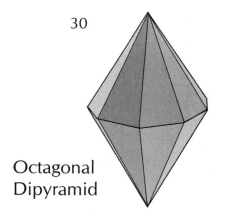

Octagonal
Dipyramid

Antidiamonds (and a Dual)

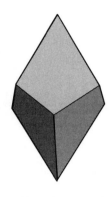

Medium Triangular Trapezohedron
page 70

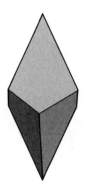

Thin Triangular Antidiamond
page 73

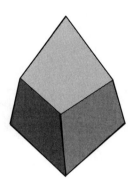

Wide Triangular Trapezohedron
page 66

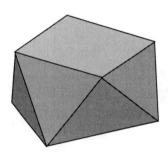

Square Antiprism
(The dual of the Square Trapezohedron)
page 76

Square Trapezohedron
page 79

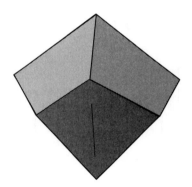

Square Trapezohedron in a Sphere
page 84

Antidiamonds, or trapezohedra, resemble diamonds where the sides are staggered around the center. The faces of each model are identical and kite shaped where three of the angles are the same. A triangular trapezohedron has three sides on top and three below. This is a collection of triangular and square antidiamonds and also a dual pair as the dual of an antidiamond is an antiprism.

These triangular antidiamonds vary from wide to thin. The square trapezohedron is the dual of the square antiprism. The wider square trapezohedron can be inscribed in a sphere. The triangular antidiamond inscribed in a sphere would be a cube and its dual would be the octahedron.

Trapezohedron	Angle a
Cube	90°
Wide Triangular	72°
Medium Triangular	60°
Thin Triangular	48°
Square	54°
Square in Sphere	65.5°

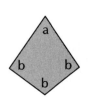

Wide Triangular Trapezohedron

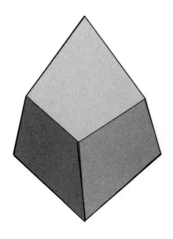

On each side of this trapezohedron, one vertex is 72° and the other three are 96°. The folds which establish this geometry are made in steps 1–13, following a folding sequence determined using Robert Lang's Reference Finder software. This model has odd symmetry.

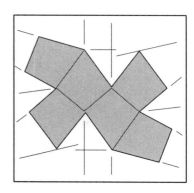

1

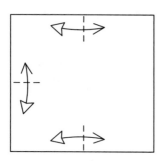

Fold and unfold at the centers of three edges.

2

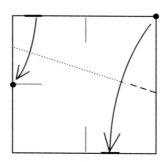

Bring the top right corner to the bottom edge and the top edge to the left center. Only crease on the right.

3

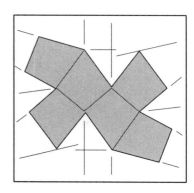

Unfold.

4

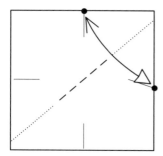

Fold and unfold, creasing in the center.

5

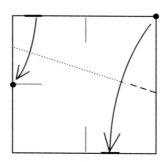

Fold and unfold diagonally in half, creasing lightly.

6

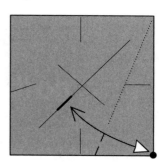

Fold and unfold to the center, creasing at the bottom.

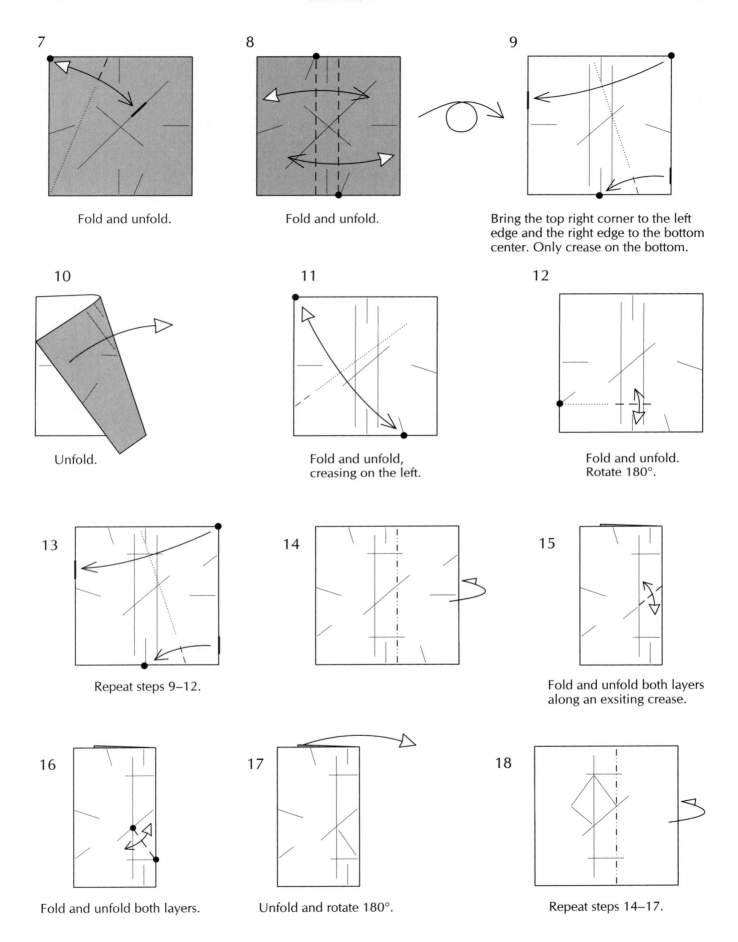

7

Fold and unfold.

8

Fold and unfold.

9

Bring the top right corner to the left edge and the right edge to the bottom center. Only crease on the bottom.

10

Unfold.

11

Fold and unfold, creasing on the left.

12

Fold and unfold. Rotate 180°.

13

Repeat steps 9–12.

14

15

Fold and unfold both layers along an exsiting crease.

16

Fold and unfold both layers.

17

Unfold and rotate 180°.

18

Repeat steps 14–17.

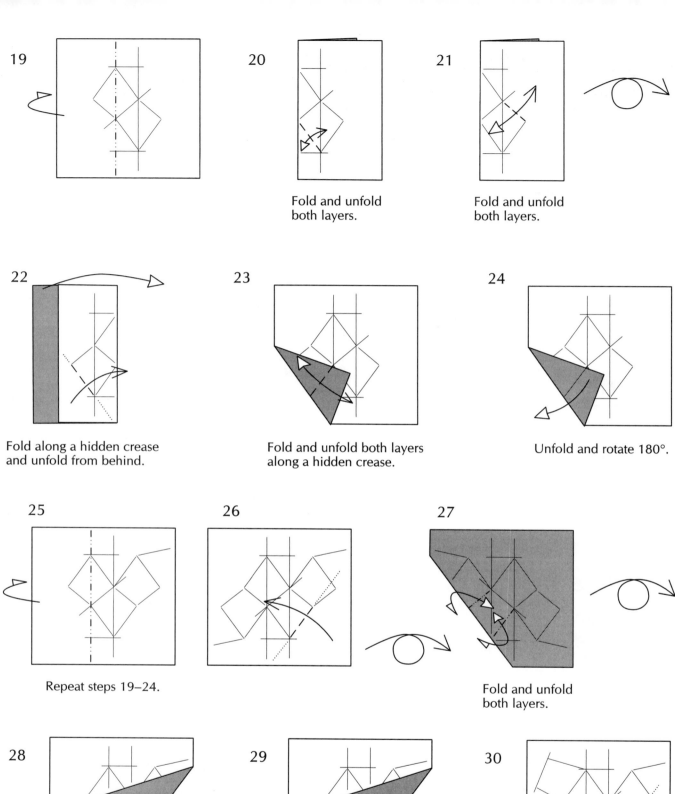

19

20

Fold and unfold
both layers.

21

Fold and unfold
both layers.

22

Fold along a hidden crease
and unfold from behind.

23

Fold and unfold both layers
along a hidden crease.

24

Unfold and rotate 180°.

25

Repeat steps 19–24.

26

27

Fold and unfold
both layers.

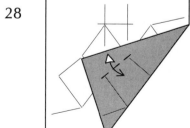

28

Fold and unfold one layer
along a hidden crease.

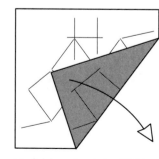

29

Unfold and rotate 180°.

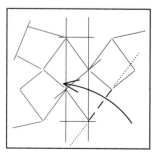

30

Repeat steps 26–29.

31

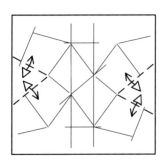

Fold and unfold, extending the creases to the edge.

32

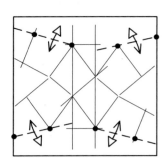

Fold and unfold, extending the creases.

33

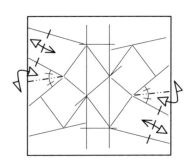

Fold and unfold.

34

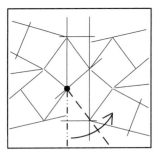

Push in at the dot as the model becomes three-dimensional.

35

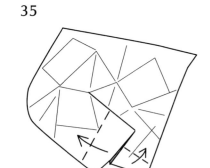

Squash-fold.

36

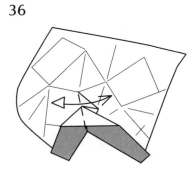

Fold and unfold.

37

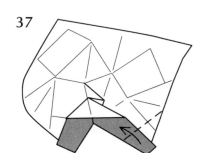

38

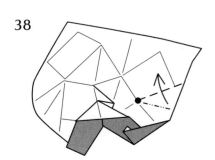

Push in at the dot.

39

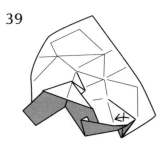

40

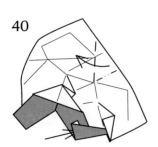

Note the pocket at the bottom. Repeat steps 34–39 above. Rotate to view the outside.

41

Tuck the two flaps inside the pockets.

42

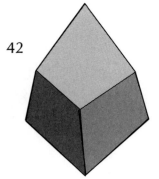

Wide Triangular Trapezohedron

Medium Triangular Trapezohedron

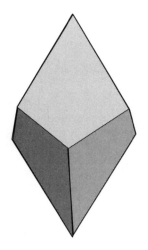

On each side of this trapezohedron, one vertex is 60° and the other three are 100°. The folds which establish this geometry are made in steps 1–9, following a folding sequence determined using Robert Lang's Reference Finder software. This model has odd symmetry. The folding method is similar to the previous trapezohedron.

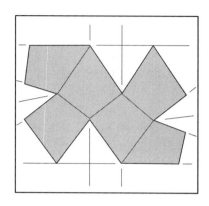

1

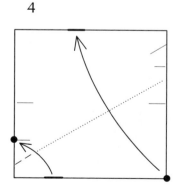

Fold in half on two sides, making small marks.

2

Bring the bottom right corner to the top edge and the bottom edge to the 1/4 mark on the left. Only crease on the left.

3

Unfold and rotate 180°.

4

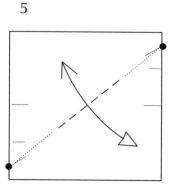

Repeat steps 2–3.

5

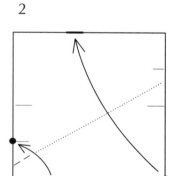

Fold and unfold, creasing in the center.

6

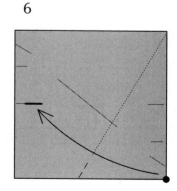

Bring the bottom right corner to the center line near the left side, creasing on the bottom.

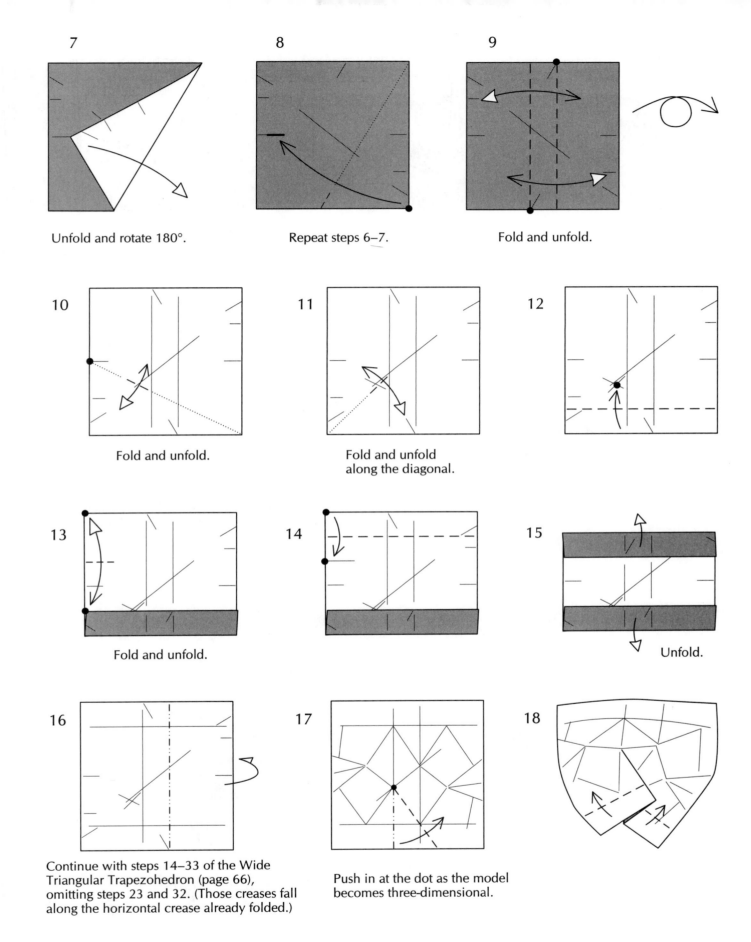

7

Unfold and rotate 180°.

8

Repeat steps 6–7.

9

Fold and unfold.

10

Fold and unfold.

11

Fold and unfold
along the diagonal.

12

13

Fold and unfold.

14

15

Unfold.

16

Continue with steps 14–33 of the Wide
Triangular Trapezohedron (page 66),
omitting steps 23 and 32. (Those creases fall
along the horizontal crease already folded.)

17

Push in at the dot as the model
becomes three-dimensional.

18

19

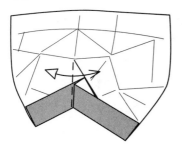

Fold and unfold.

20

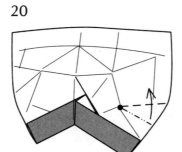

Push in at the dot.

21

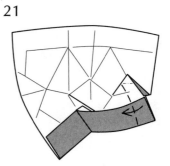

Squash-fold.

22

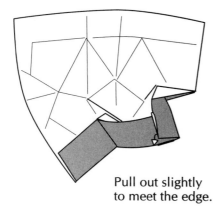

Pull out slightly
to meet the edge.

23

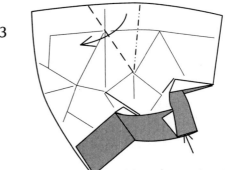

Note the pocket. Repeat
steps 17–22 above. Rotate
to view the outside.

24

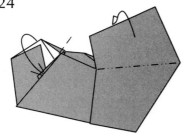

Tuck the two flaps
inside the pockets.

25

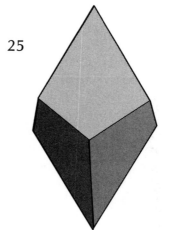

Medium Triangular
Trapezohedron

Thin Triangular Trapezohedron

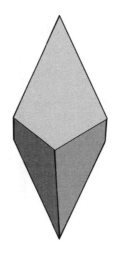

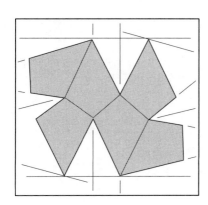

On each side of this antidiamond, one vertex is 48° and the other three are 104°. The folds which establish this geometry are made in steps 1–11, following a folding sequence determined using Robert Lang's Reference Finder software. This model has odd symmetry. The folding method is similar to the previous trapezohedra.

1

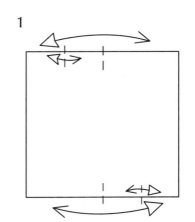

Fold in half on two sides, making small marks.

2

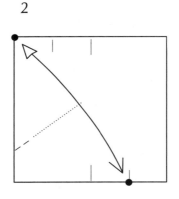

Fold and unfold, creasing at the left.

3

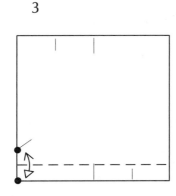

Fold and unfold. Rotate 180°.

4

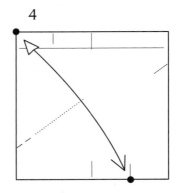

Repeat steps 2–3.

5

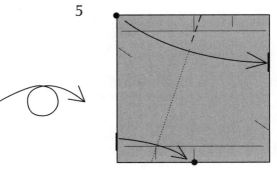

Bring the top left corner to the right edge and the left edge to the bottom center. Only crease on the top.

6

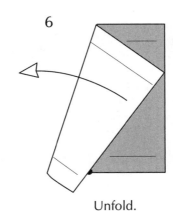

Unfold.

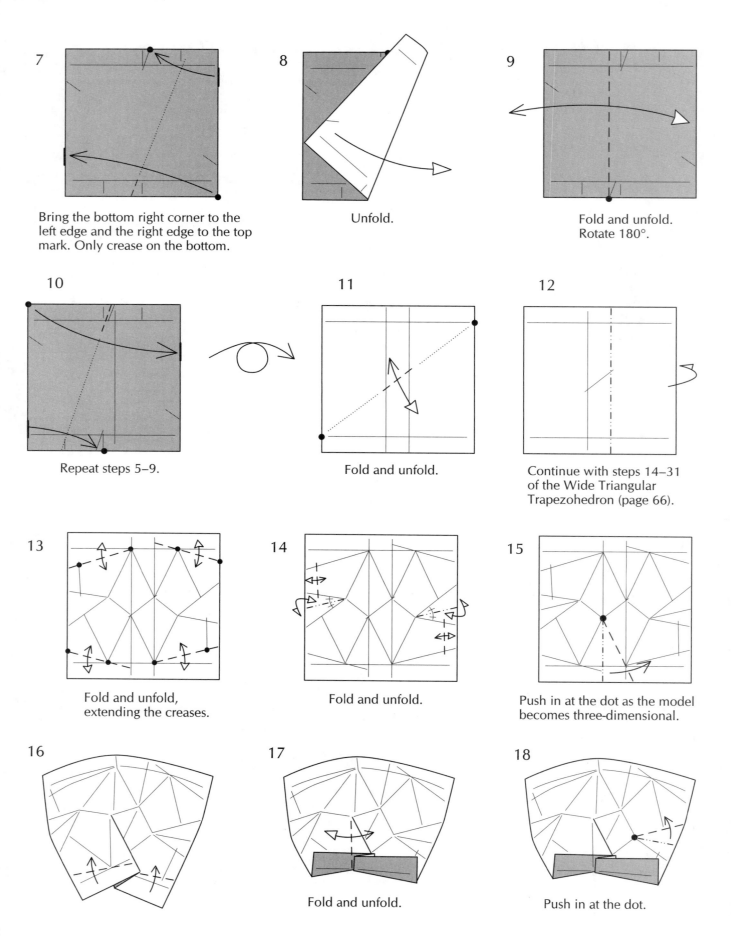

7 Bring the bottom right corner to the left edge and the right edge to the top mark. Only crease on the bottom.

8 Unfold.

9 Fold and unfold. Rotate 180°.

10 Repeat steps 5–9.

11 Fold and unfold.

12 Continue with steps 14–31 of the Wide Triangular Trapezohedron (page 66).

13 Fold and unfold, extending the creases.

14 Fold and unfold.

15 Push in at the dot as the model becomes three-dimensional.

16

17 Fold and unfold.

18 Push in at the dot.

19

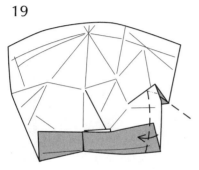

Squash-fold.

20

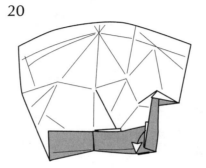

Pull out slightly
to meet the edge.

21

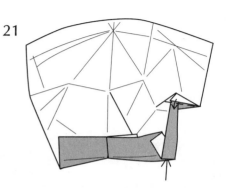

Note the pocket. (This step,
with the valley fold at the
middle right side, is optional.)

22

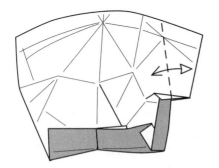

Fold and unfold.
Rotate 180°.

23

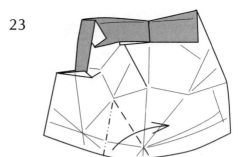

Repeat steps 15–22.

24

Tuck the two flaps
inside the pockets.

25

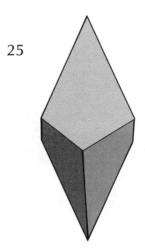

Thin Triangular Antidiamond

Square Antiprism

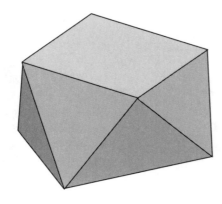 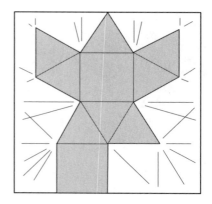

A prism has two identical polygons on opposite sides connected by rectangles. The opposite sides of an antiprism are connected by triangles. As the dual of the prism is the diamond, the dual of an antiprism is an antidiamond.

This antiprism is composed of two squares and eight equilateral triangles. Its dual is the square trapezohedron (next model). The folding follows even symmetry (whatever is done on the left is repeated on the right) until near the end.

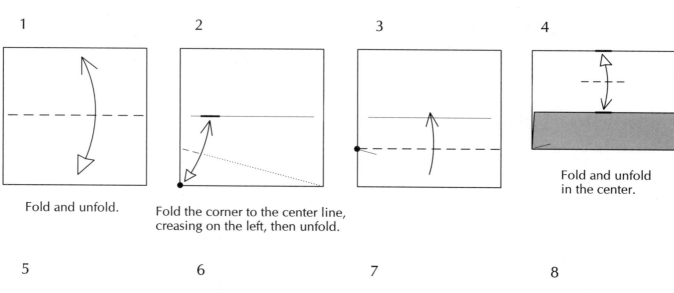

1

Fold and unfold.

2

Fold the corner to the center line, creasing on the left, then unfold.

3

4

Fold and unfold in the center.

5

Unfold.

6

Fold and unfold at the bottom and just at the top.

7

Fold and unfold.

8

Fold and unfold.

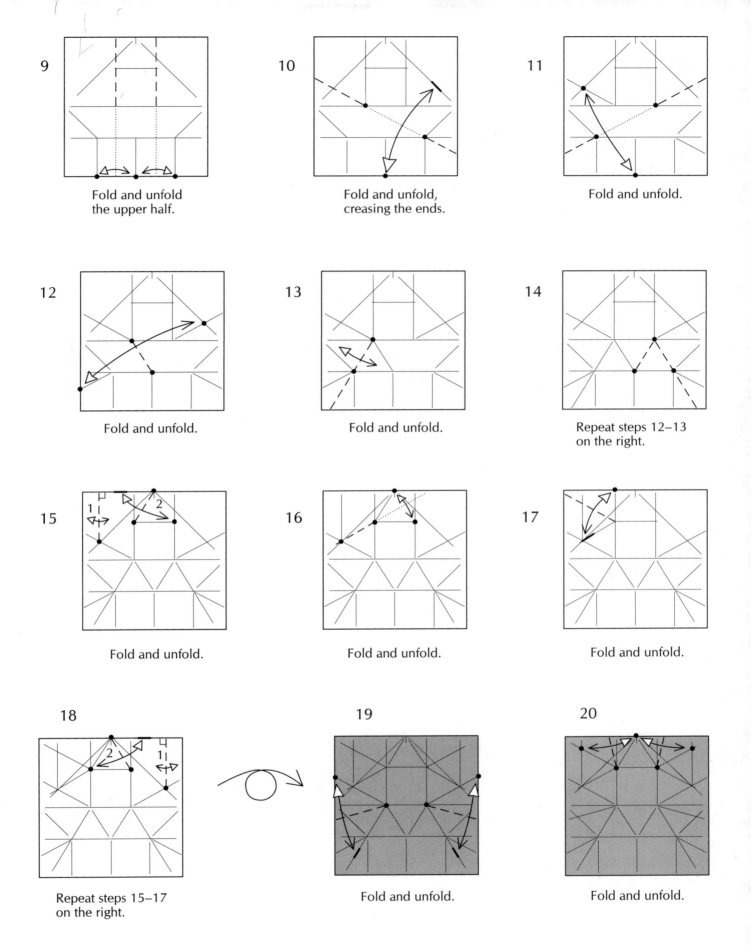

9   Fold and unfold
the upper half.

10   Fold and unfold,
creasing the ends.

11   Fold and unfold.

12   Fold and unfold.

13   Fold and unfold.

14   Repeat steps 12–13
on the right.

15   Fold and unfold.

16   Fold and unfold.

17   Fold and unfold.

18   Repeat steps 15–17
on the right.

19   Fold and unfold.

20   Fold and unfold.

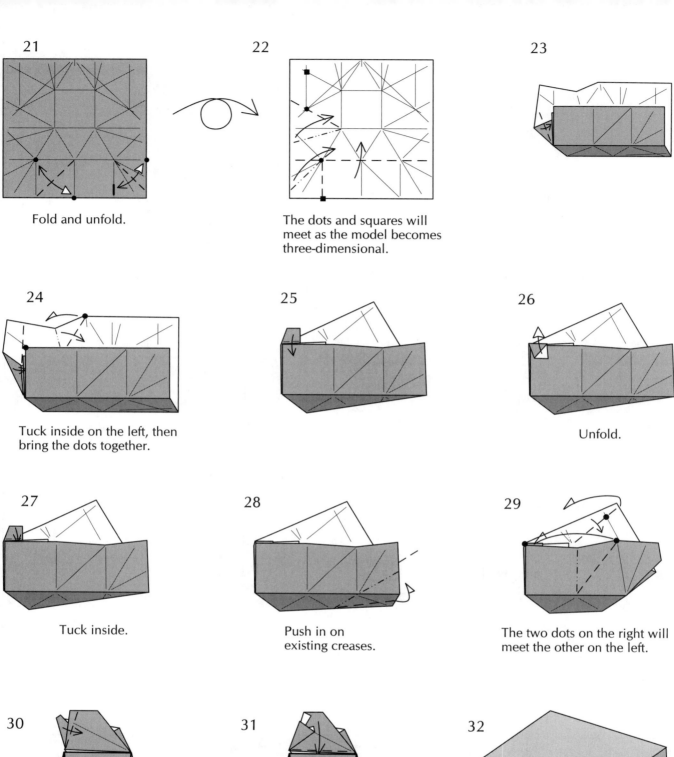

21

Fold and unfold.

22

The dots and squares will meet as the model becomes three-dimensional.

23

24

Tuck inside on the left, then bring the dots together.

25

26

Unfold.

27

Tuck inside.

28

Push in on existing creases.

29

The two dots on the right will meet the other on the left.

30

There are eight triangles going around two squares at the top and bottom, along with a tab of several layers. Fold all the layers of the tab together.

31

Tuck inside to lock the model.

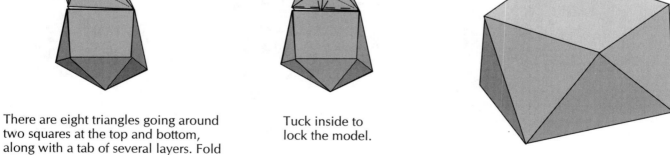

32

Square Antiprism

Square Trapezohedron

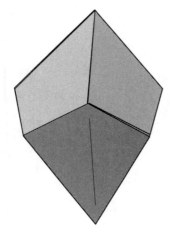

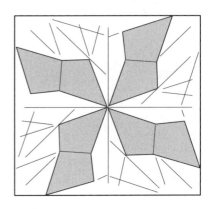

This antidiamond is the dual of the square antiprism with equilateral triangles (previous model). The crease pattern shows it uses square symmetry. On each side, one angle is 54°, the three other ones are 102°. The model closes with a twist lock which is similar to the lock in the octahedron. The folds which establish this model's geometry are made in steps 3–8, following a folding sequence determined using Robert Lang's Reference Finder software.

1

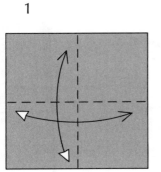

Fold and unfold.

2

Fold and unfold
along the diagonals.

3

Bring the top right corner to the bottom edge and the top edge to the left center. Only crease on the left.

4

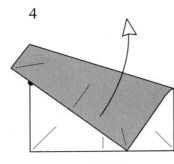

Unfold.

5

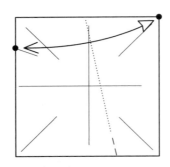

Fold and unfold creasing
only at the bottom.

6

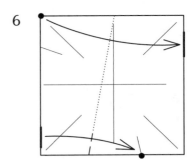

Bring the top left corner to the right edge and the left edge to the dot at the bottom. Only crease on the bottom.

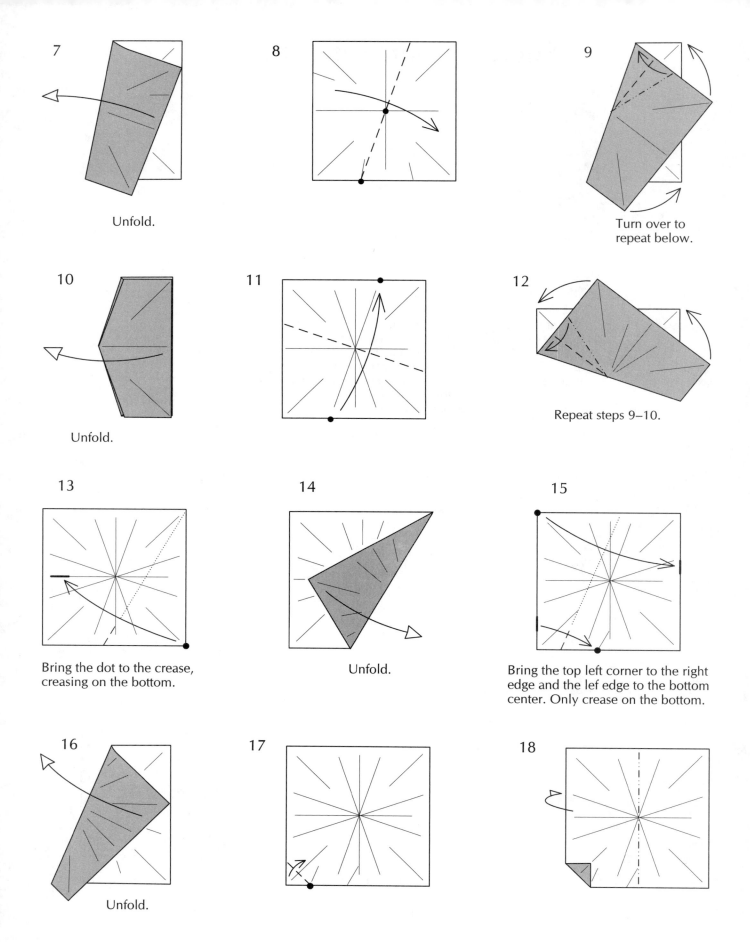

7

Unfold.

8

9

Turn over to repeat below.

10

Unfold.

11

12

Repeat steps 9–10.

13

Bring the dot to the crease, creasing on the bottom.

14

Unfold.

15

Bring the top left corner to the right edge and the lef edge to the bottom center. Only crease on the bottom.

16

Unfold.

17

18

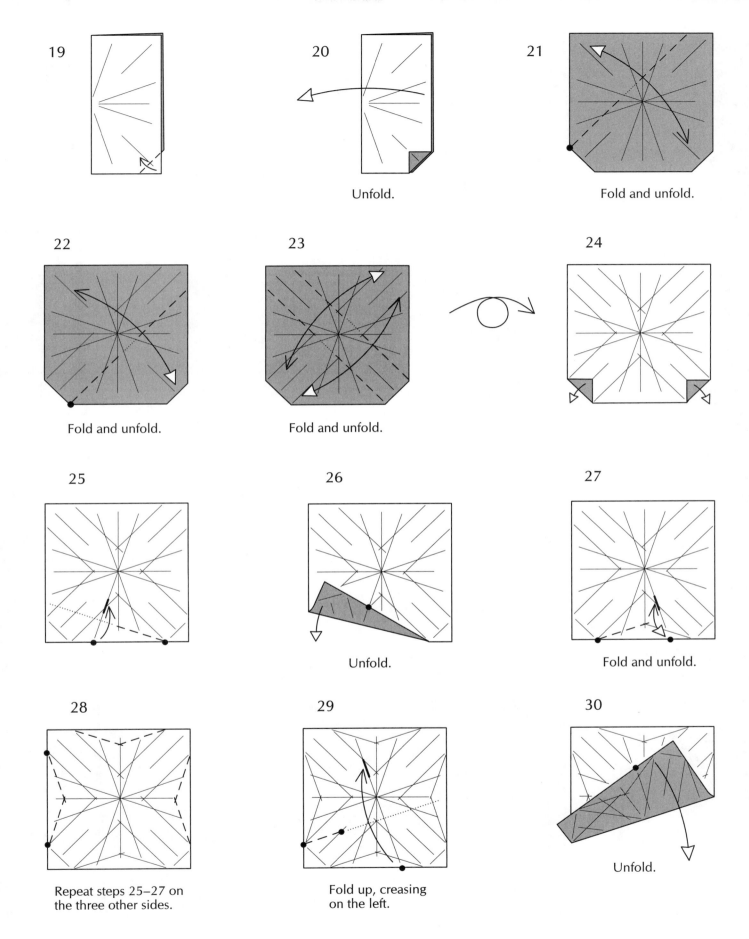

19

20

Unfold.

21

Fold and unfold.

22

Fold and unfold.

23

Fold and unfold.

24

25

26

Unfold.

27

Fold and unfold.

28

Repeat steps 25–27 on the three other sides.

29

Fold up, creasing on the left.

30

Unfold.

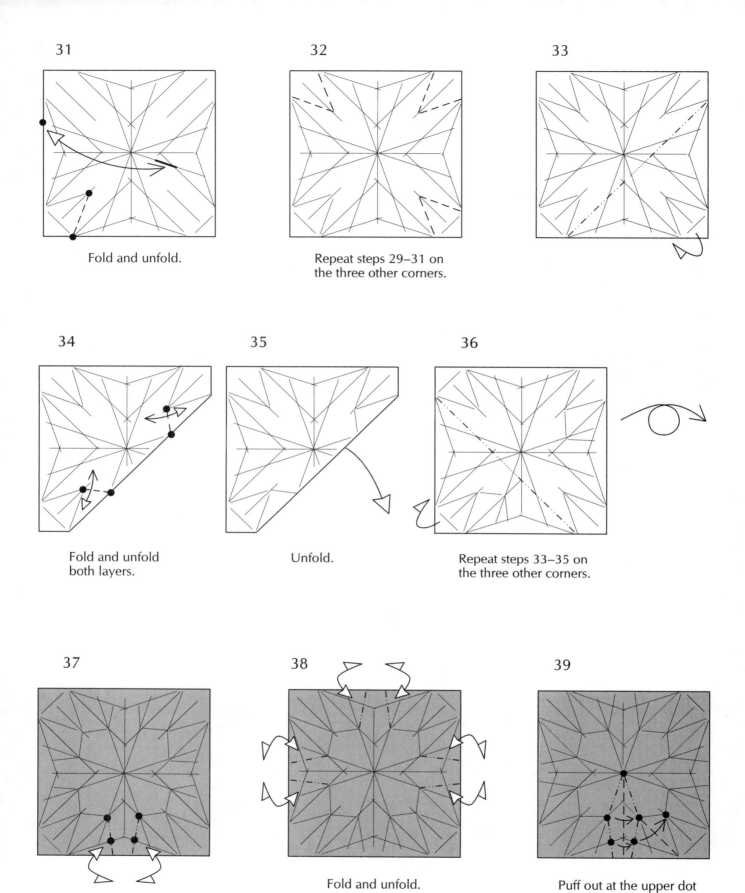

31

Fold and unfold.

32

Repeat steps 29–31 on
the three other corners.

33

34

Fold and unfold
both layers.

35

Unfold.

36

Repeat steps 33–35 on
the three other corners.

37

Fold and unfold.

38

Fold and unfold.

39

Puff out at the upper dot
as the model becomes
three-dimensional.

40

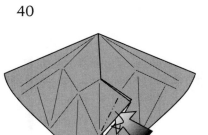

Reverse-fold locking several layers by the top.

41

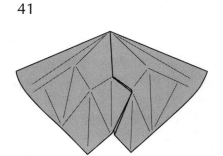

Repeat steps 39–40 on the three other corners.

42

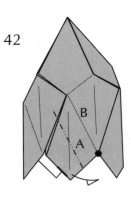

Mountain-fold line A so the edge meets the dot. Lines A and B are roughly parallel.

43

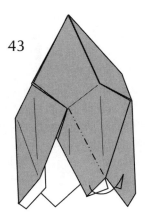

44

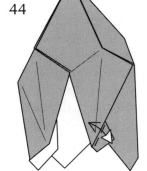

Fold and unfold the tab.

45

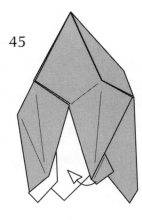

Unfold.

46

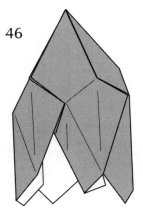

Repeat steps 42–45 on the three other corners.

47

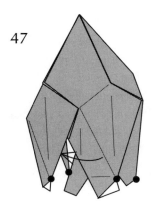

Tuck the tab inside. Repeat all around so the four dots meet at the bottom with a twist lock.

48

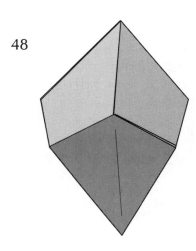

Square Trapezohedron

Square Trapezohedron in a Sphere

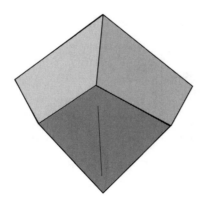

This is the square trapezohedron which is inscribed in a sphere—each of the vertices would meet at the surface of a sphere. The acute angle in each side is about 65.5°. The folding method is similar to the previous trapezohedron. The folds which establish this model's geometry are made in steps 3–8, following a folding sequence determined using Robert Lang's Reference Finder software.

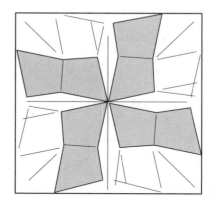

1

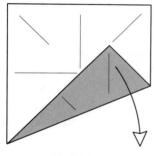

Fold and unfold.

2

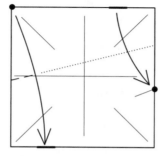

Fold and unfold along the diagolnals.

3

Bring the bottom edge to the center, creasing on the right.

4

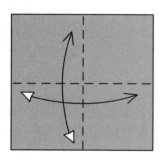

Unfold.

5

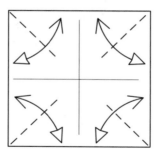

Bring the top left corner to the bottom edge and the top edge to the dot at the right. Only crease on the left.

6

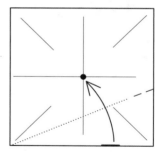

Unfold.

7

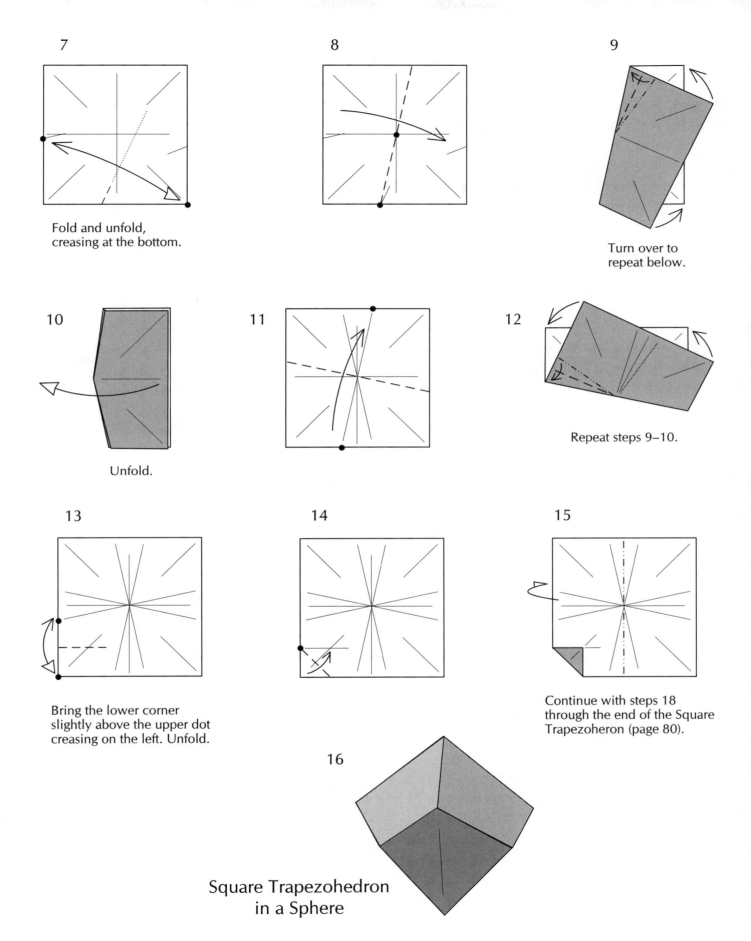

Fold and unfold,
creasing at the bottom.

8

Turn over to
repeat below.

9

10

Unfold.

11

12

Repeat steps 9–10.

13

Bring the lower corner
slightly above the upper dot
creasing on the left. Unfold.

14

15

Continue with steps 18
through the end of the Square
Trapezoheron (page 80).

16

Square Trapezohedron
in a Sphere

Sunken Shapes

**Dimpled Truncated
Octahedron**
page 87

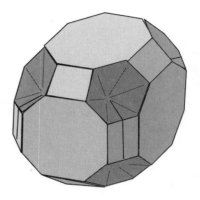

**Dimpled Great
Rhombicuboctahedron**
page 90

These models are sunken versions of Archimedean solids. Archimedean solids, or semiregular solids, have faces of several types of regular polygons with identical corners. These shapes can be inscribed in a sphere. All of these have square symmetry.

These sunken shapes make for an interesting and challenging collection.

Dimpled Snub Cube
page 94

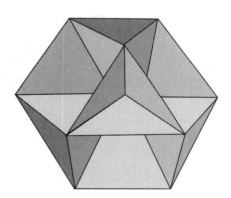

Sunken Cuboctahedron
page 99

Dimpled Truncated Octahedron

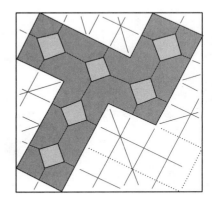

The dimpled truncated octahedron has eight sunken hexagons and six square sides. In the crease pattern the darker shade refers to the sunken hexagons. This uses square symmetry though 1/4 is hidden.

1

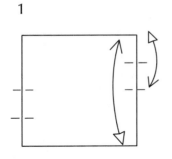

Make small marks by folding and unfolding in quarters.

2

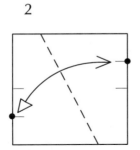

Fold and unfold.

3

Fold and unfold.

4

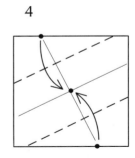

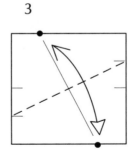

5

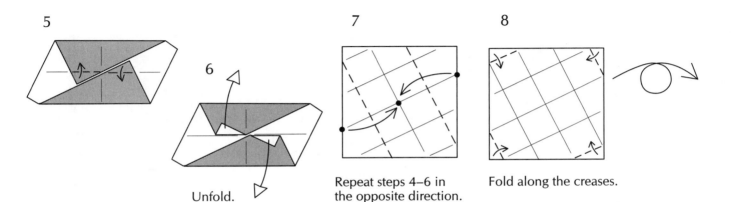

6

Unfold.

7

Repeat steps 4–6 in the opposite direction.

8

Fold along the creases.

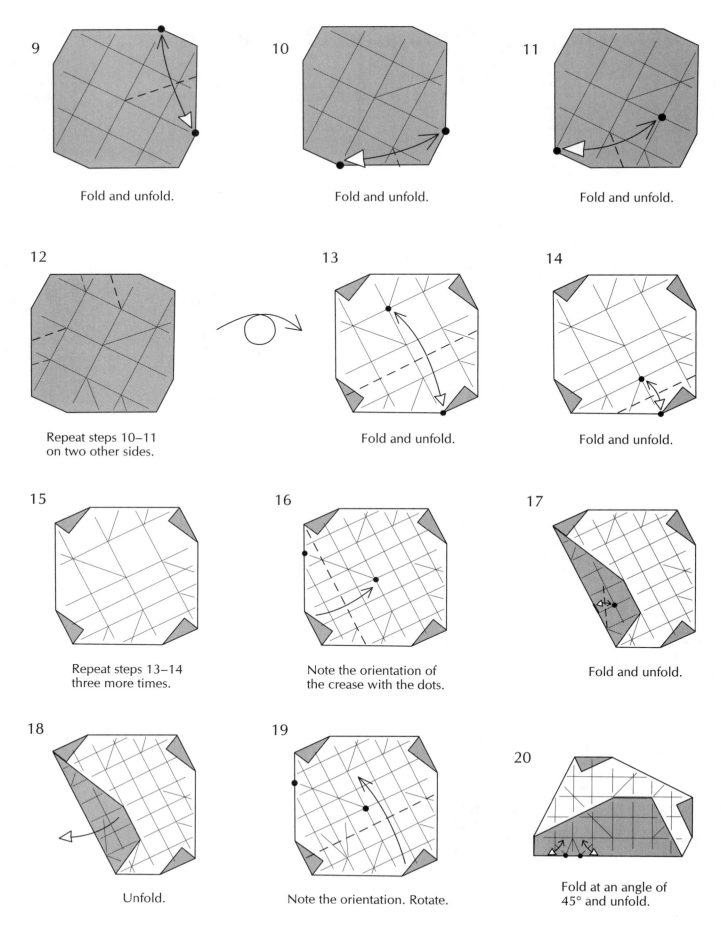

9 Fold and unfold.

10 Fold and unfold.

11 Fold and unfold.

12 Repeat steps 10–11 on two other sides.

13 Fold and unfold.

14 Fold and unfold.

15 Repeat steps 13–14 three more times.

16 Note the orientation of the crease with the dots.

17 Fold and unfold.

18 Unfold.

19 Note the orientation. Rotate.

20 Fold at an angle of 45° and unfold.

21

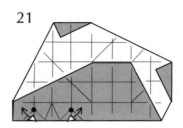

Fold and unfold.

22

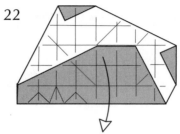

Unfold and rotate.

23

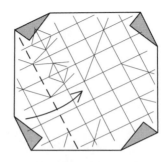

Repeat steps 16–22.

24

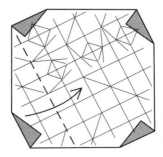

Repeat steps 16–22.

25

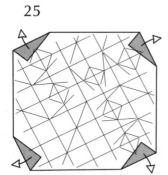

Note the six
diamonds. Unfold.

26

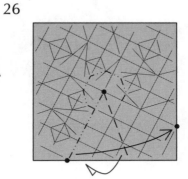

Push in at the center to
form a sunken hexagon.

27

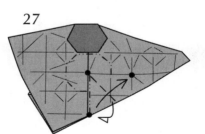

Push in at the center to
form a sunken hexagon.

28

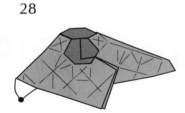

Rotate to view the dot.

29

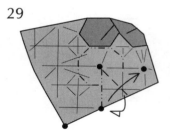

Repeat steps 27–28
two more times.

30

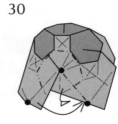

Push in at the
center to form a
sunken hexagon.

31

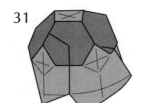

Repeat step 30
two more times.

32

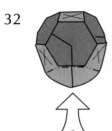

Form the last sunken hexagon by
folding and interlocking the three
flaps that meet at the bottom.

33

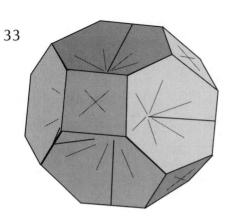

Dimpled Truncated Octahedron

Dimpled Great Rhombicuboctahedron

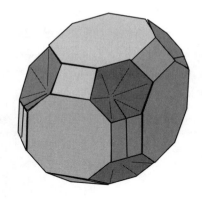

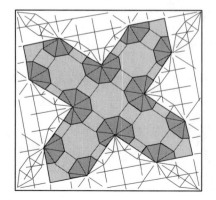

The great rhombicuboctahedron resembles a shaved cube. It has six octahedrons, eight hexagons, and twelve squares. For this dimpled one, the hexagons are sunken. The darker part of the crease pattern is for the sunken hexagons. This model develops as an ornamented cube.

1

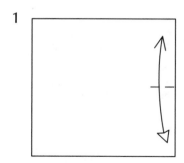

Fold and unfold.

2

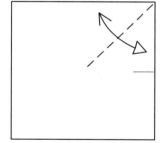

Fold and unfold.

3

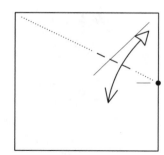

Fold and unfold, creasing along the diagonal.

4

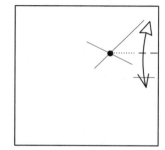

Fold and unfold. This divides the paper in thirds.

5

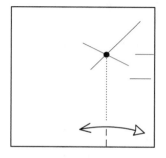

Fold and unfold.

6

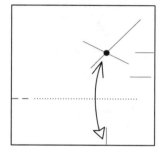

Fold and unfold.

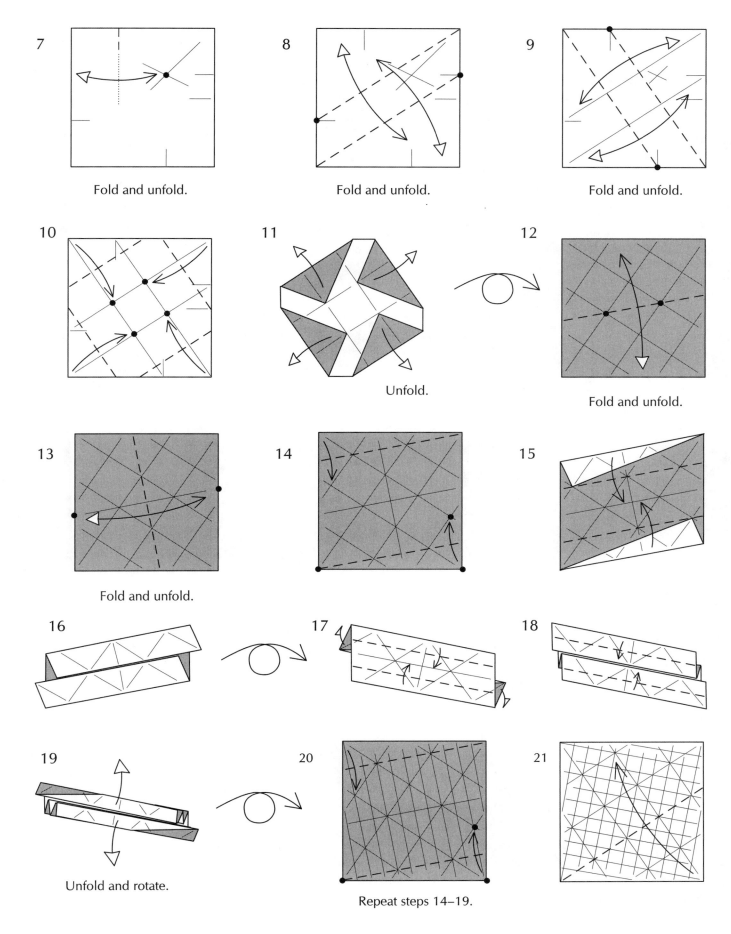

7 Fold and unfold.

8 Fold and unfold.

9 Fold and unfold.

10

11 Unfold.

12 Fold and unfold.

13 Fold and unfold.

14

15

16

17

18

19 Unfold and rotate.

20 Repeat steps 14–19.

21

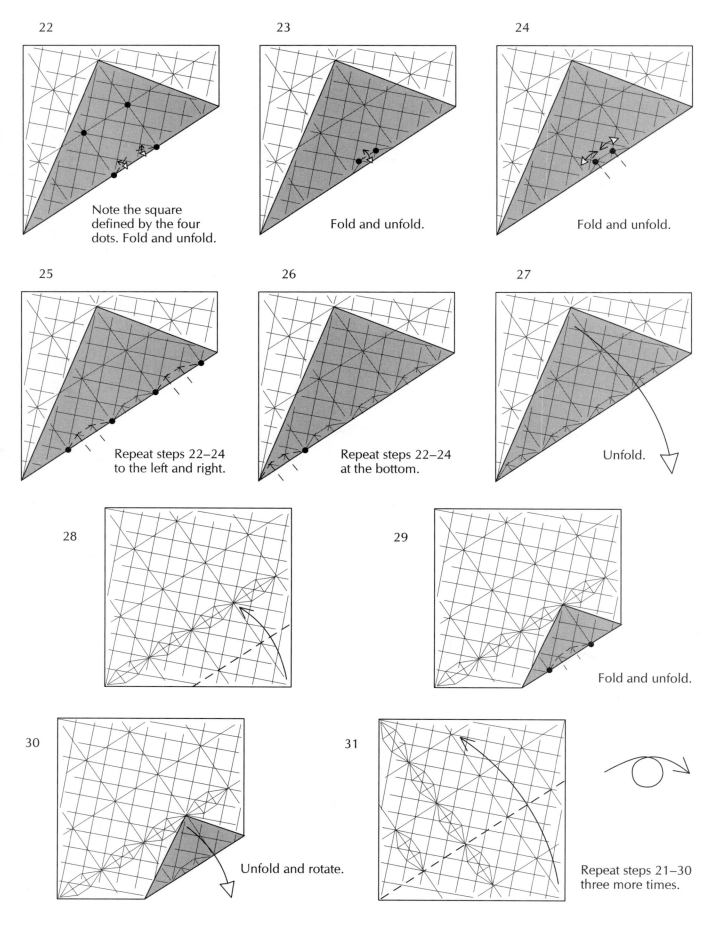

22

Note the square defined by the four dots. Fold and unfold.

23

Fold and unfold.

24

Fold and unfold.

25

Repeat steps 22–24 to the left and right.

26

Repeat steps 22–24 at the bottom.

27

Unfold.

28

29

Fold and unfold.

30

Unfold and rotate.

31

Repeat steps 21–30 three more times.

32

Push in at the dot in the center to form a sunken hexagon and bring the other dots together as the model becomes three-dimensional.

33

Fold and unfold close to the sunken hexagon.

34

Repeat steps 32–33 three more times.

35

Rotate the top to the bottom and bring the dot to the center.

36

Push in at the dot in the center to form a sunken hexagon and bring the other dots together.

37

Unfold and rotate.

38

Repeat steps 36–37 three more times.

39

Refold and repeat behind on the opposite corner.

40

Fold on opposite corners.

41

Refold along the creases. Push in on the left and right to form sunken hexagons, and tuck inside at the top to lock the model. Rotate.

42

Dimpled Great Rhombicuboctahedron

Dimpled Great Rhombicuboctahedron 93

Dimpled Snub Cube

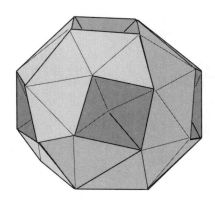

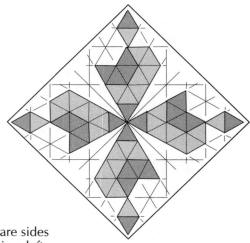

This polyhedron has six indented square sides and 32 equilateral triangles. It comes in a left and right handed form. The crease pattern shows the model has square symmetry. The darker areas refer to the sunken squares.

1

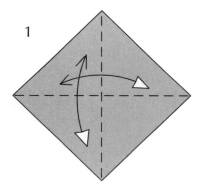

Fold and unfold along the diagonals. Rotate.

2

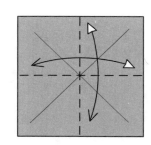

Fold and unfold.

3

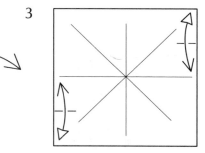

Fold and unfold to make quarter marks.

4

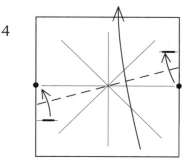

Align the dots and lines on the front and back.

5

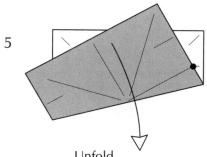

Unfold.

6

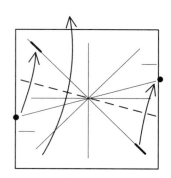

Align the dots and lines on the front and back.

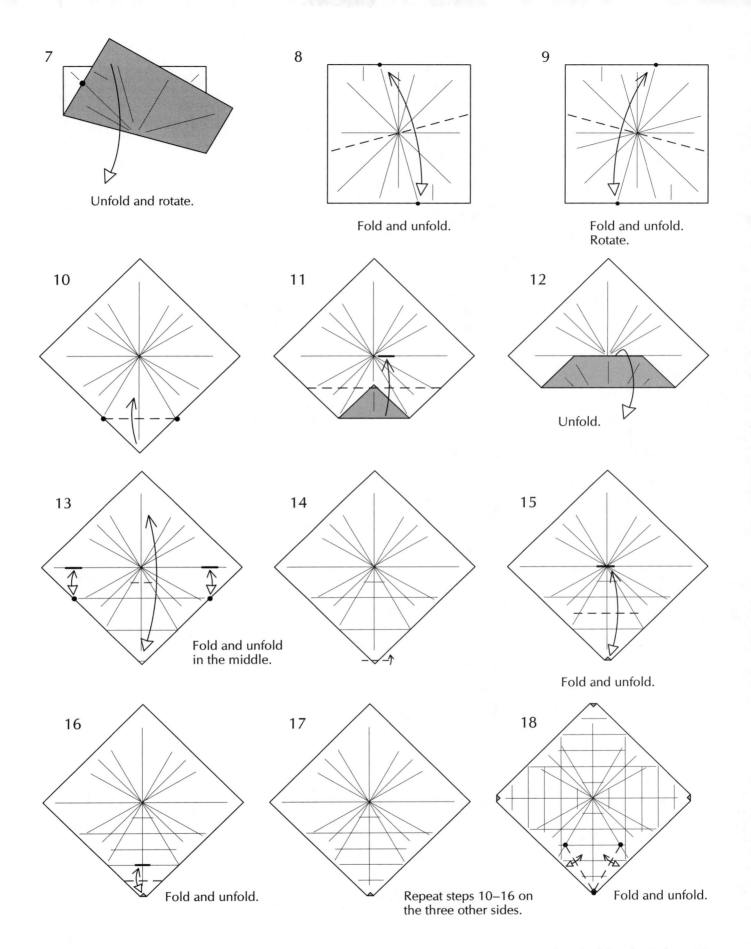

7

Unfold and rotate.

8

Fold and unfold.

9

Fold and unfold.
Rotate.

10

11

12

Unfold.

13

Fold and unfold
in the middle.

14

15

Fold and unfold.

16

Fold and unfold.

17

Repeat steps 10–16 on
the three other sides.

18

Fold and unfold.

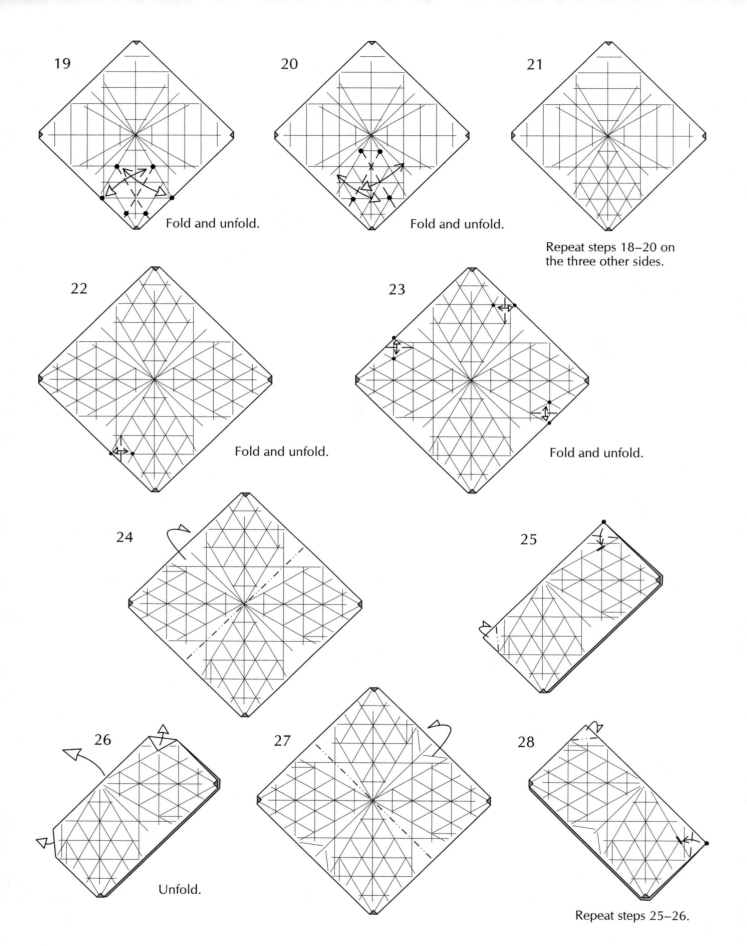

19 Fold and unfold.

20 Fold and unfold.

21 Repeat steps 18–20 on the three other sides.

22 Fold and unfold.

23 Fold and unfold.

24

25

26 Unfold.

27

28 Repeat steps 25–26.

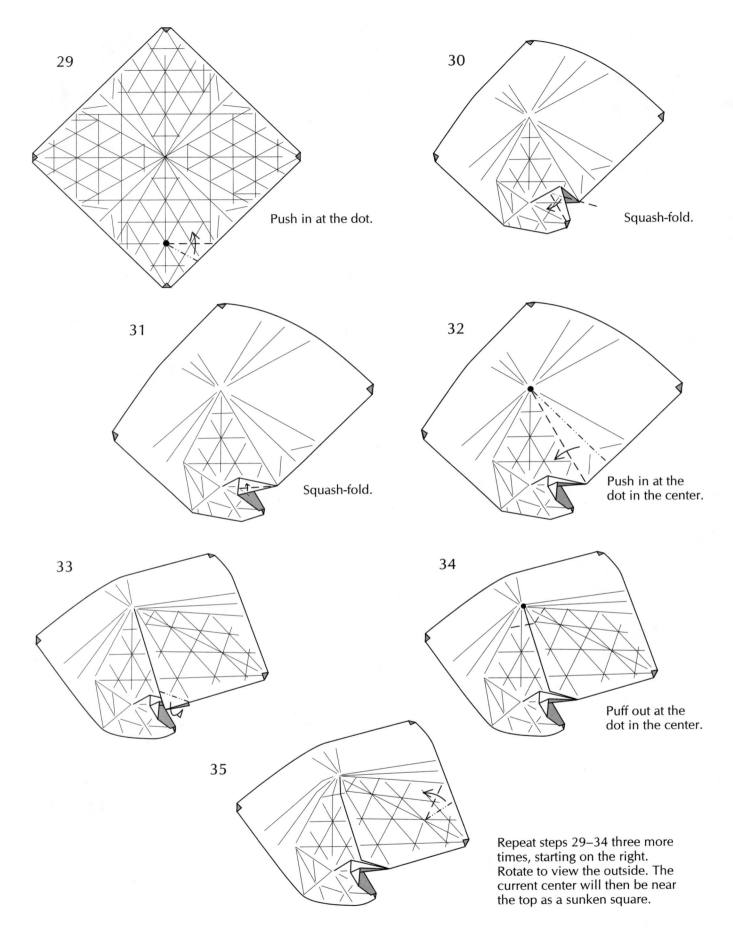

29 Push in at the dot.

30 Squash-fold.

31 Squash-fold.

32 Push in at the dot in the center.

33

34 Puff out at the dot in the center.

35 Repeat steps 29–34 three more times, starting on the right. Rotate to view the outside. The current center will then be near the top as a sunken square.

36

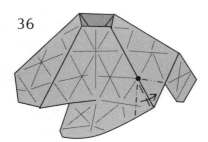

Puff out at the dot.

37

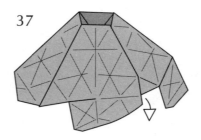

Unfold.

38

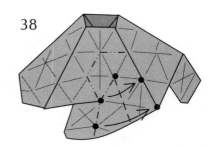

Push in at the upper dot to form a sunken square.

39

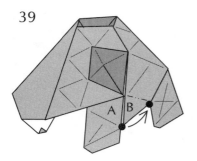

Repeat step 36 on the hidden layers so triangle A will cover triangle B.

40

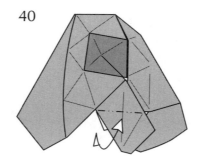

Fold and unfold.

41

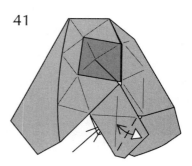

Fold and unfold. Note the pocket.

42

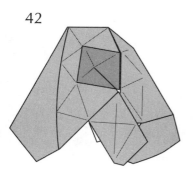

Repeat steps 36–41 three more times.

43

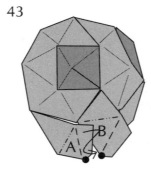

Triangles A and B are two of the four that will form the bottom sunken square. Tuck each of the flaps inside the pockets to close the model.

44

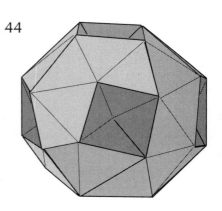

Dimpled Snub Cube

Sunken Cuboctahedron

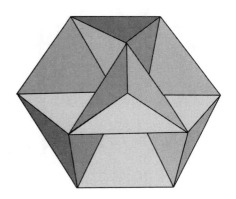

The cuboctahedron has six square and eight triangular sides. This sunken version has 48 triangular sides.

1

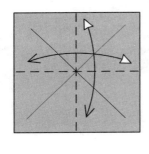

Fold and unfold along the diagonals. Rotate.

2

Fold and unfold.

3

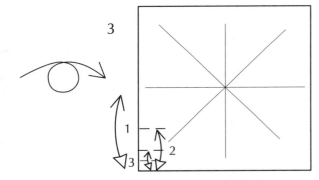

Fold and unfold in half three times.

4

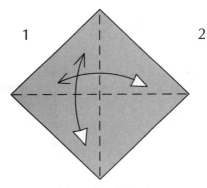

Rotate.

5

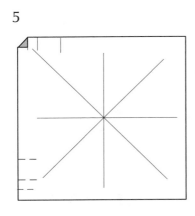

Repeat steps 3–4 three more times. Turn over and rotate.

6

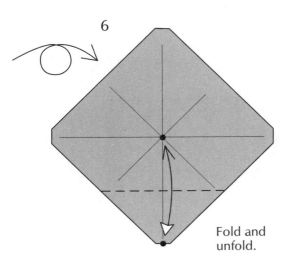

Fold and unfold.

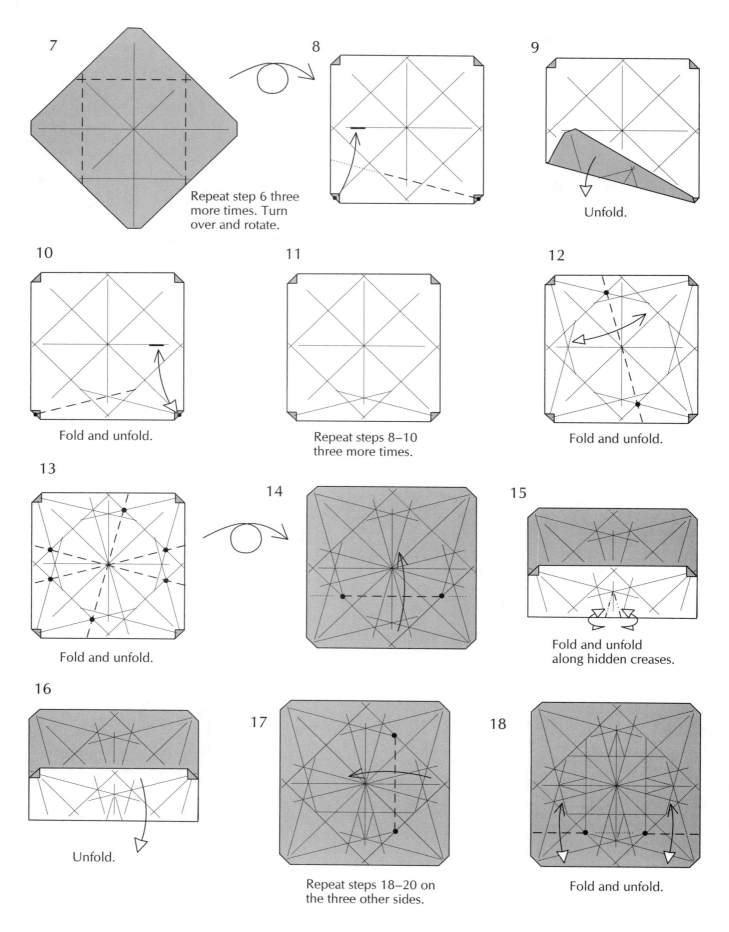

7

Repeat step 6 three more times. Turn over and rotate.

8

9

Unfold.

10

Fold and unfold.

11

Repeat steps 8–10 three more times.

12

Fold and unfold.

13

Fold and unfold.

14

15

Fold and unfold along hidden creases.

16

Unfold.

17

Repeat steps 18–20 on the three other sides.

18

Fold and unfold.

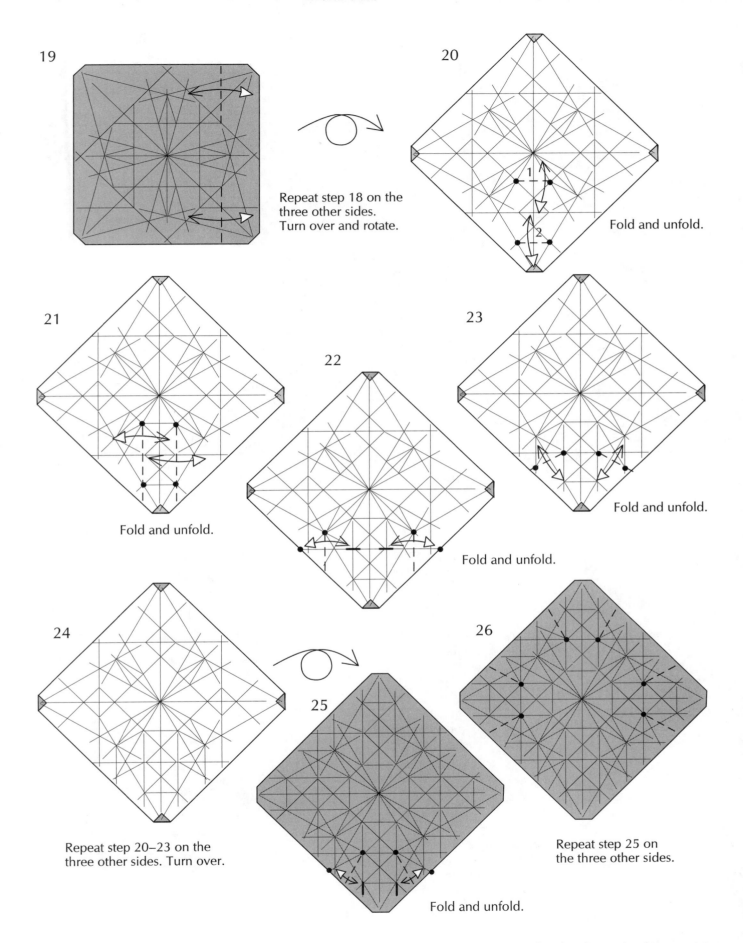

19

20

Repeat step 18 on the
three other sides.
Turn over and rotate.

1

2

Fold and unfold.

21

22

23

Fold and unfold.

Fold and unfold.

Fold and unfold.

24

25

26

Repeat step 20–23 on the
three other sides. Turn over.

Fold and unfold.

Repeat step 25 on
the three other sides.

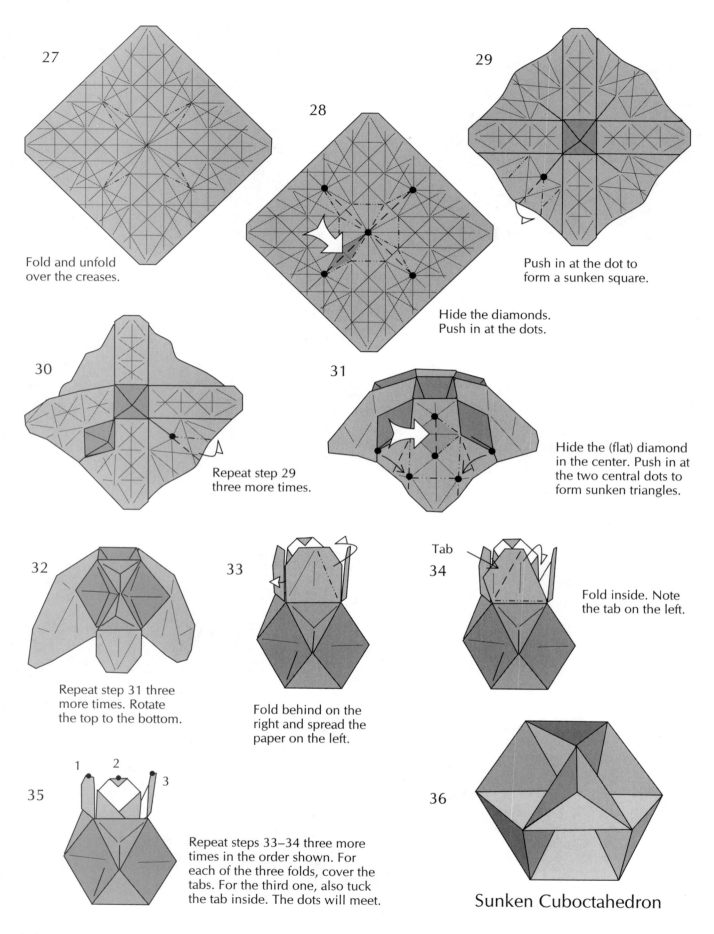

27

Fold and unfold over the creases.

28

Hide the diamonds. Push in at the dots.

29

Push in at the dot to form a sunken square.

30

Repeat step 29 three more times.

31

Hide the (flat) diamond in the center. Push in at the two central dots to form sunken triangles.

32

Repeat step 31 three more times. Rotate the top to the bottom.

33

Fold behind on the right and spread the paper on the left.

34

Tab

Fold inside. Note the tab on the left.

35

1 2 3

Repeat steps 33–34 three more times in the order shown. For each of the three folds, cover the tabs. For the third one, also tuck the tab inside. The dots will meet.

36

Sunken Cuboctahedron

Stars

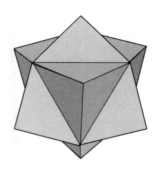

Stellated Octahedron
page 104

Omega Star
page 106

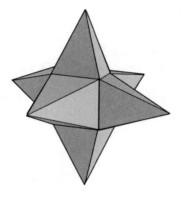

Jackstone
page 108

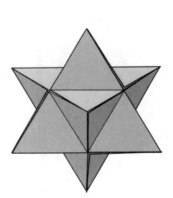

Stella Octangula
page 111

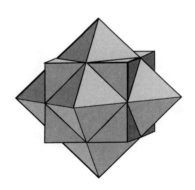

Gamma Star
page 115

These stars range from six to fourteen points. The folding for each exhibit square symmetry. That is, the crease pattern is the same when rotated 90°. This challenging collection of stellated shapes makes a very attractive display.

Stellated Octahedron

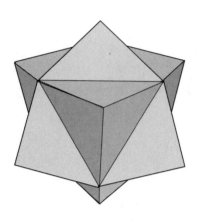

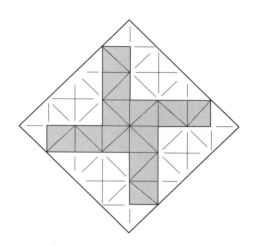

The stellated octahedron can be formed from a cube. Given a cube, valley-fold between adjacent centers. From the diagram on the right, push in to form a straight line on the valley fold line and continue all around to change a cube into a stellated octahedron.

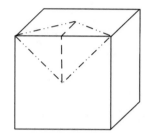

1

Fold and unfold
along the diagonals.

2

Fold and unfold.

3

Fold and unfold.

4

Fold and unfold.

5

Fold to the center and unfold.

6

Fold and unfold.

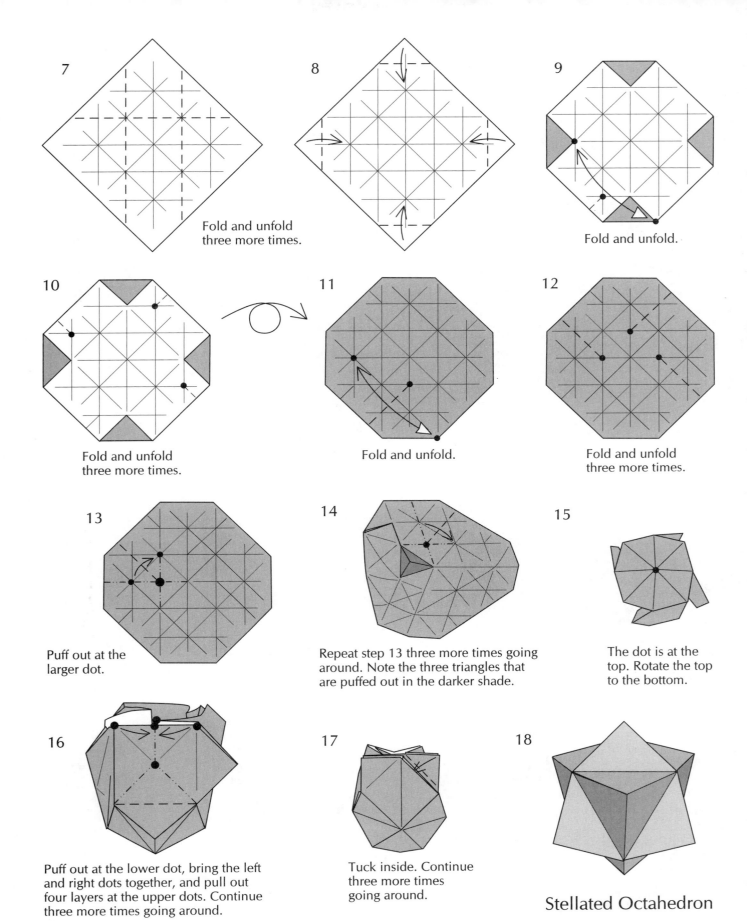

7

Fold and unfold
three more times.

8

9

Fold and unfold.

10

Fold and unfold
three more times.

11

Fold and unfold.

12

Fold and unfold
three more times.

13

Puff out at the
larger dot.

14

Repeat step 13 three more times going
around. Note the three triangles that
are puffed out in the darker shade.

15

The dot is at the
top. Rotate the top
to the bottom.

16

Puff out at the lower dot, bring the left
and right dots together, and pull out
four layers at the upper dots. Continue
three more times going around.

17

Tuck inside. Continue
three more times
going around.

18

Stellated Octahedron

Omega Star

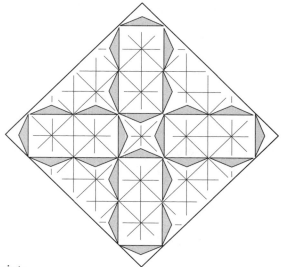

The omega star has twelve points. The geometry of the finished shape is based on a rhombic dodecahedron.

1

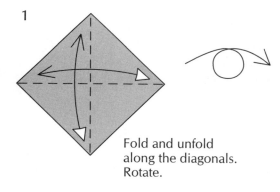

Fold and unfold along the diagonals. Rotate.

2

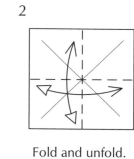

Fold and unfold.

3

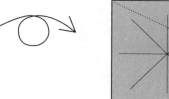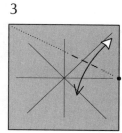

Fold and unfold, creasing at the diagonal.

4

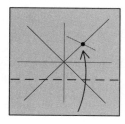

This divides the paper in thirds.

5

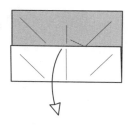

Unfold.

6

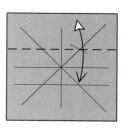

Fold and unfold.

7

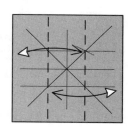

Fold and unfold.

8

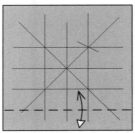

Fold and unfold.

9

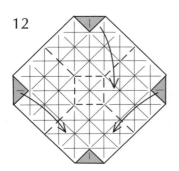

Fold and unfold.
Turn over and rotate.

10

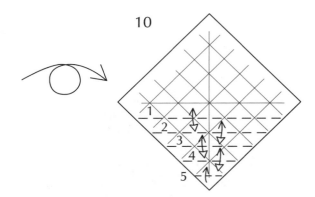

Fold and unfold starting
with the highest one. Do
not unfold the last one.

11

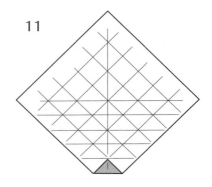

Repeat step 10 on the
three other corners.

12

13

Push in at the upper dot
to form a sunken triangle.

14

15

Repeat steps 13–14
three more times.

16

Spread at the bottom to
form a sunken triangle.

17

Repeat step 16
three more times.

18

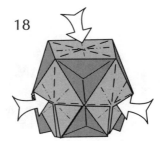

Sink the sides first, then
the top. Repeat all around.

19

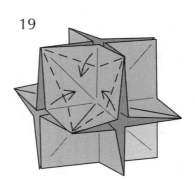

Fold inward.

20

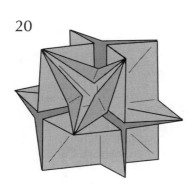

Repeat step 19 all around.

21

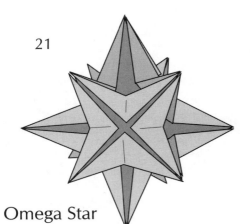

Omega Star

Jackstone

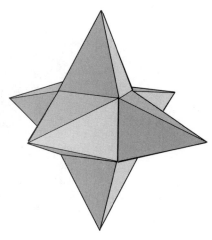

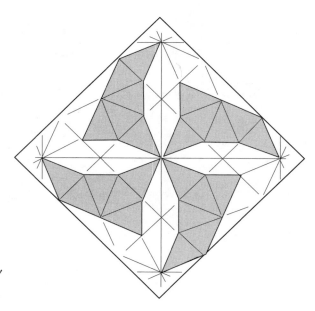

A few decades ago, origami pioneer Jack Skillman designed this model from a single square, using a double blintz frog base. His contribution brought origami to a new level. Knowing his model, I sought to compose the largest possible one from a given size. Simultaneously, origami creator Sy Chen designed this jackstone using the same crease pattern.

The jackstone is composed of six square pyramids around a cube. The angle at the tips of each pyramid is 45°.

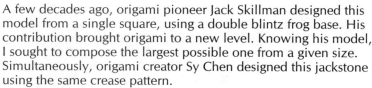

1

Fold and unfold along the diagonals.

2

Fold and unfold.

3

Fold to the landmarks and turn over to check the landmarks on the back.

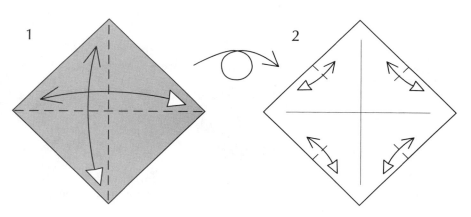

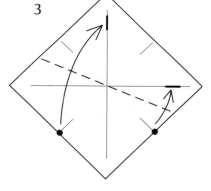

4

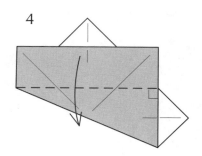

5

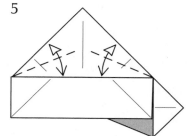

Fold and unfold.

6

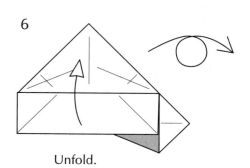

Unfold.

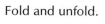

7

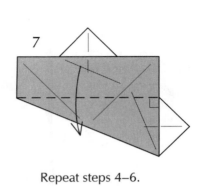

Repeat steps 4–6.

8

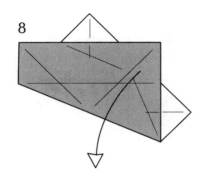

Unfold and rotate.

9

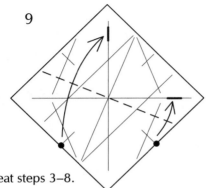

Repeat steps 3–8.

10

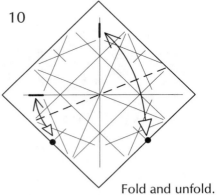

Fold and unfold.

11

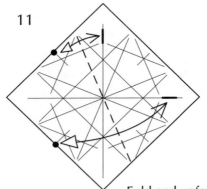

Fold and unfold.

12

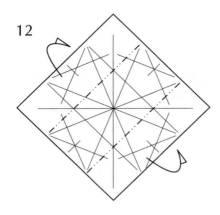

13

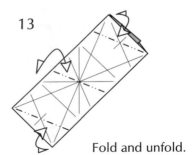

Fold and unfold.

14

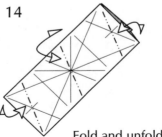

Fold and unfold.

15

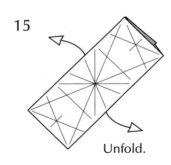

Unfold.

16

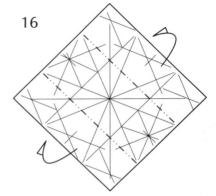

Repeat steps 12–15 in the other direction.

17

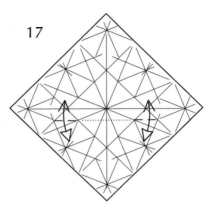

Fold and unfold.

18

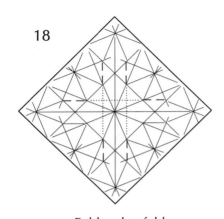

Fold and unfold.

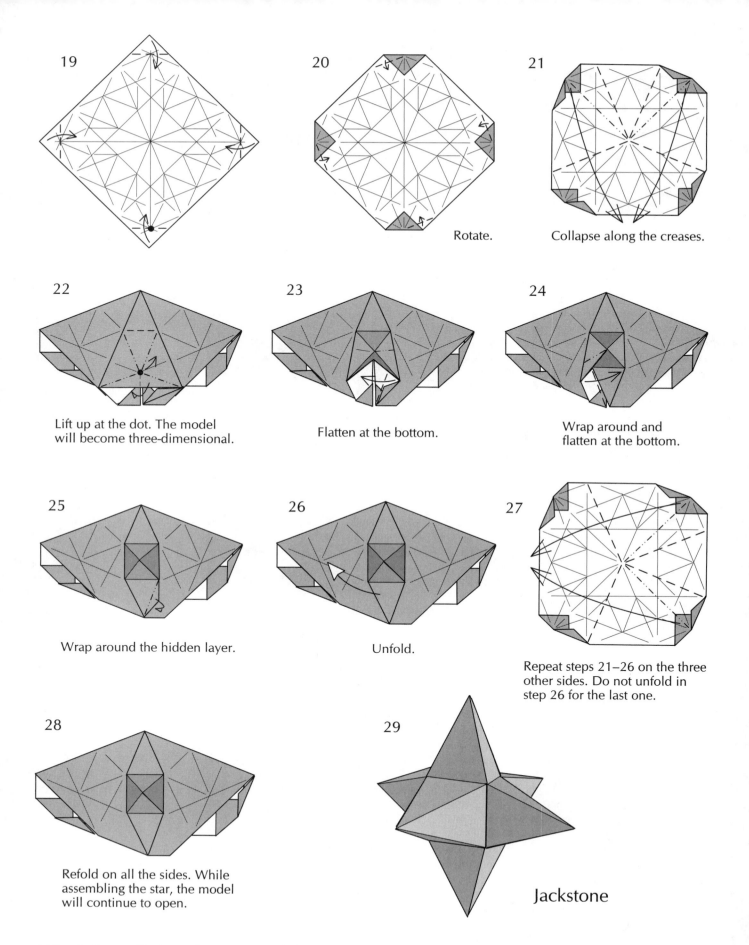

19

20

Rotate.

21

Collapse along the creases.

22

Lift up at the dot. The model
will become three-dimensional.

23

Flatten at the bottom.

24

Wrap around and
flatten at the bottom.

25

Wrap around the hidden layer.

26

Unfold.

27

Repeat steps 21–26 on the three
other sides. Do not unfold in
step 26 for the last one.

28

Refold on all the sides. While
assembling the star, the model
will continue to open.

29

Jackstone

Stella Octangula

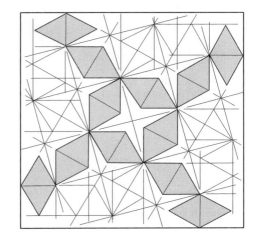

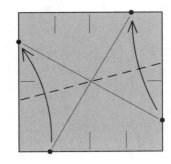

All the sides of this eight-pointed star are equilateral triangles. This shape can be viewed as two intersecting tetrahedra, or eight tetrahedra on the faces of an octahedron. It can be formed by taking a cube and collapsing along an "X" on each side.

1

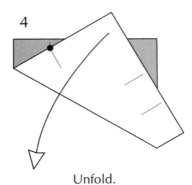

Fold in half on two sides, making small marks.

2

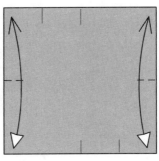

Fold and unfold making small marks.

3

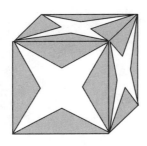

Align the dots and lines on the front and back.

4

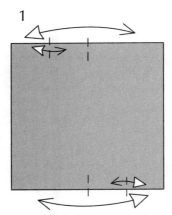

Unfold.

5

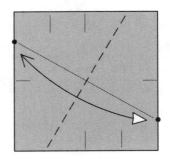

Fold and unfold.

6

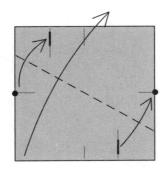

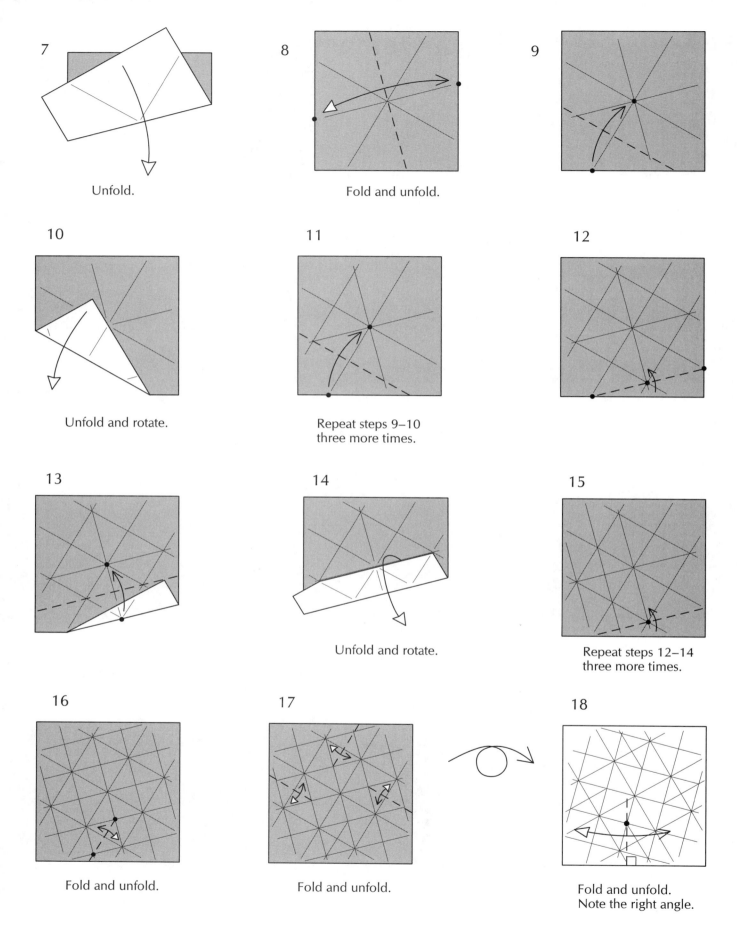

7 Unfold.

8 Fold and unfold.

9

10 Unfold and rotate.

11 Repeat steps 9–10 three more times.

12

13

14 Unfold and rotate.

15 Repeat steps 12–14 three more times.

16 Fold and unfold.

17 Fold and unfold.

18 Fold and unfold. Note the right angle.

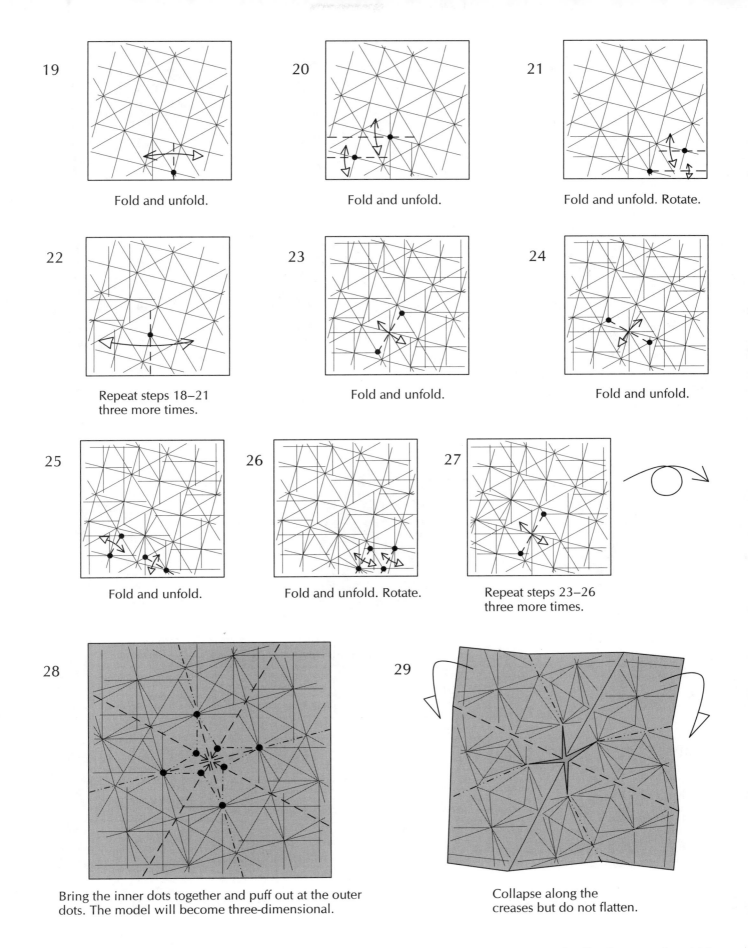

19 Fold and unfold.

20 Fold and unfold.

21 Fold and unfold. Rotate.

22 Repeat steps 18–21 three more times.

23 Fold and unfold.

24 Fold and unfold.

25 Fold and unfold.

26 Fold and unfold. Rotate.

27 Repeat steps 23–26 three more times.

28 Bring the inner dots together and puff out at the outer dots. The model will become three-dimensional.

29 Collapse along the creases but do not flatten.

30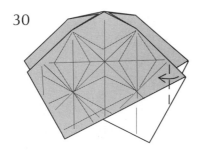

31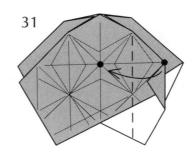

32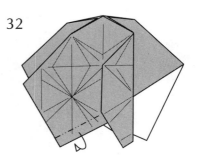

33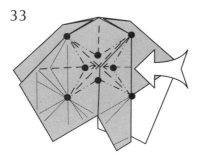

Bring the inner dots together and puff out at the outer dots. Open on the right.

34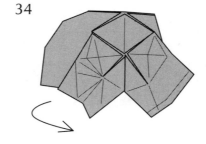

Rotate.

35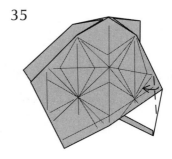

Repeat steps 30–34 three more times.

36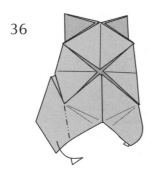

Repeat three more times going around. Rotate the top to the bottom.

37

Repeat three more times going around. Four sides meet at the dot.

38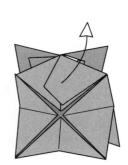

Unfold on all four sides.

39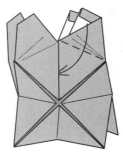

Tuck inside. Repeat all around and rotate.

40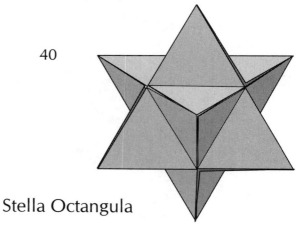

Stella Octangula

Gamma star

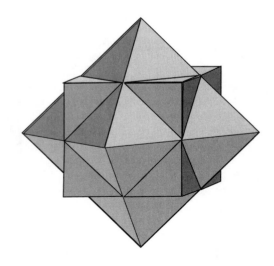

This challenging model can be viewed as a cube and octahedron intersecting. The crease pattern shows it is designed from an octahedron with triangular pyramids coming out of each of the eight faces.

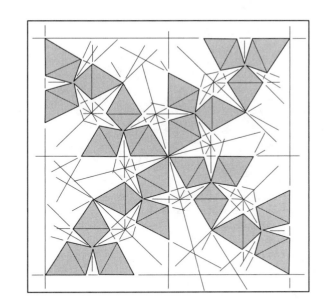

1

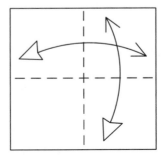

Fold and unfold.

2

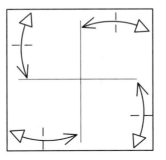

Fold and unfold.

3

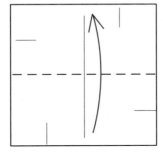

4

Turn over and repeat.

5

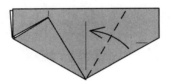

Turn over and repeat.

6

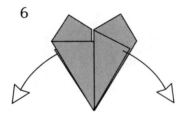

Unfold.

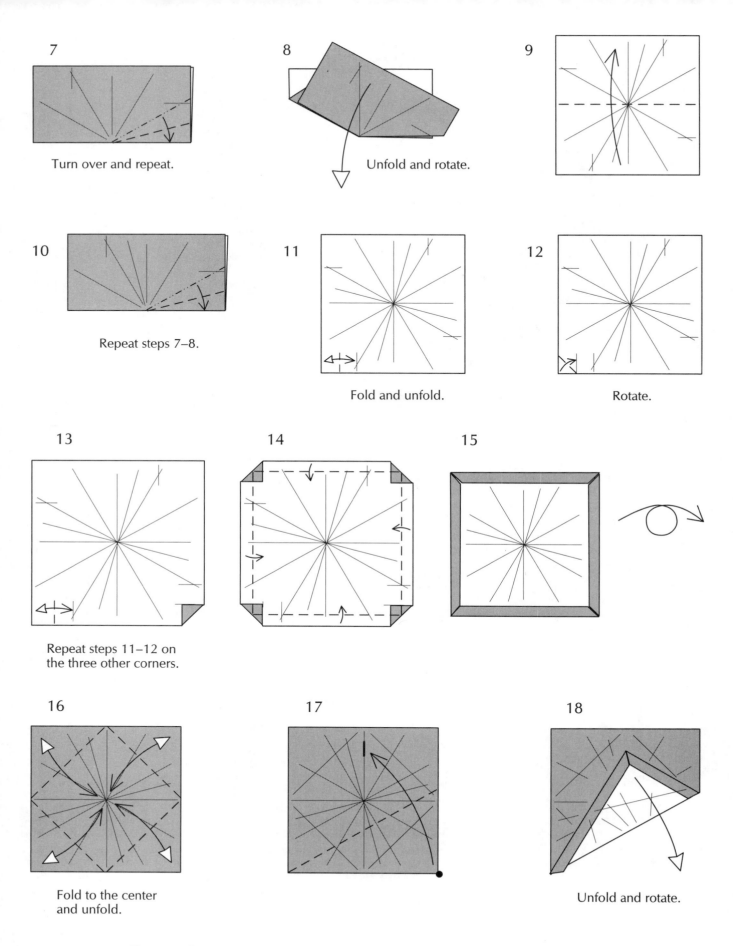

7

Turn over and repeat.

8

Unfold and rotate.

9

10

Repeat steps 7–8.

11

Fold and unfold.

12

Rotate.

13

Repeat steps 11–12 on
the three other corners.

14

15

16

Fold to the center
and unfold.

17

18

Unfold and rotate.

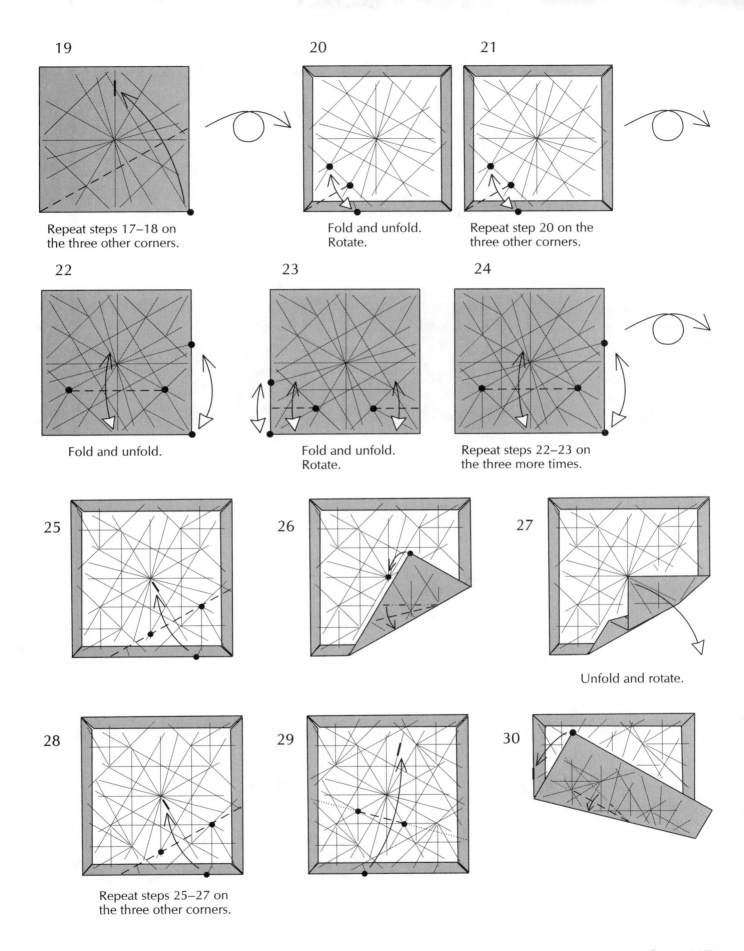

19

Repeat steps 17–18 on the three other corners.

20

Fold and unfold. Rotate.

21

Repeat step 20 on the three other corners.

22

Fold and unfold.

23

Fold and unfold. Rotate.

24

Repeat steps 22–23 on the three more times.

25

26

27

Unfold and rotate.

28

Repeat steps 25–27 on the three other corners.

29

30

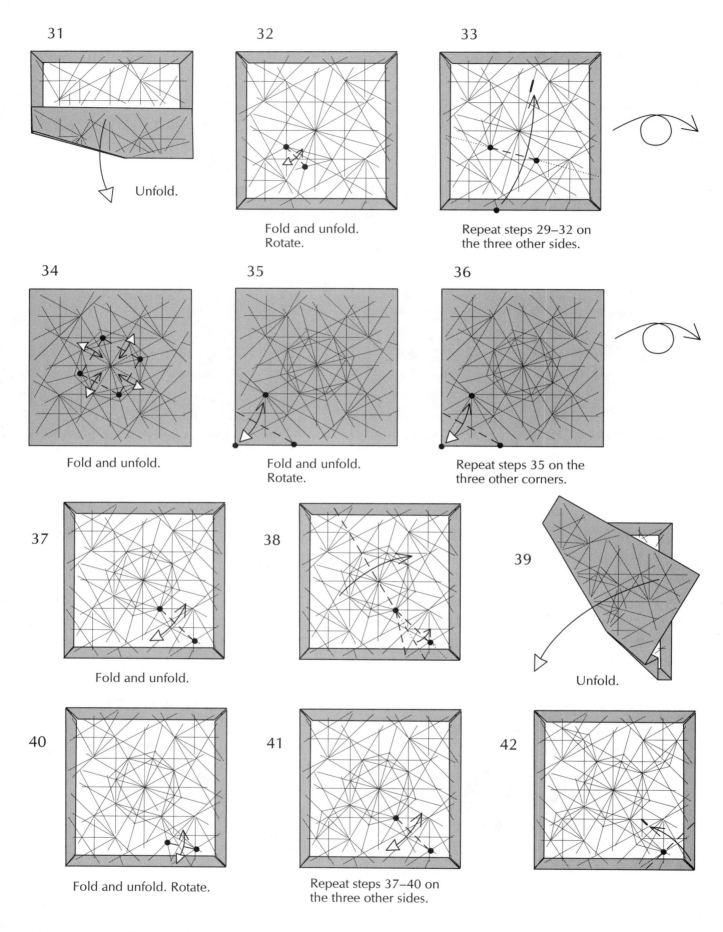

31

Unfold.

32

Fold and unfold.
Rotate.

33

Repeat steps 29–32 on
the three other sides.

34

Fold and unfold.

35

Fold and unfold.
Rotate.

36

Repeat steps 35 on the
three other corners.

37

Fold and unfold.

38

39

Unfold.

40

Fold and unfold. Rotate.

41

Repeat steps 37–40 on
the three other sides.

42

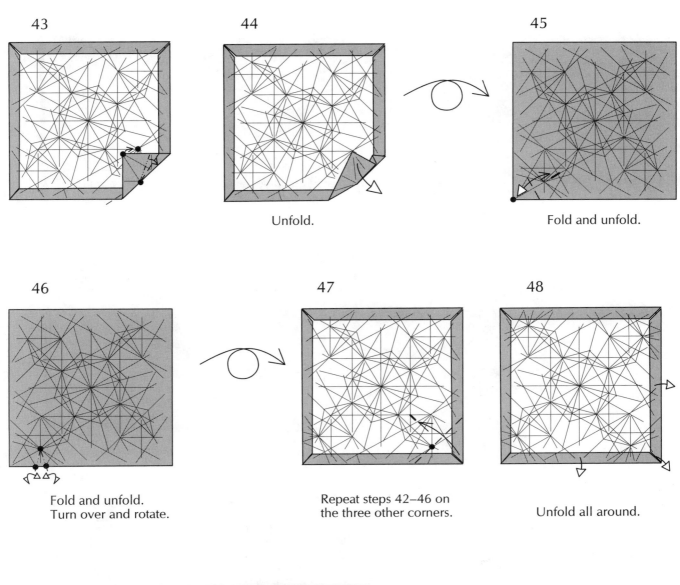

43

44

Unfold.

45

Fold and unfold.

46

Fold and unfold.
Turn over and rotate.

47

Repeat steps 42–46 on
the three other corners.

48

Unfold all around.

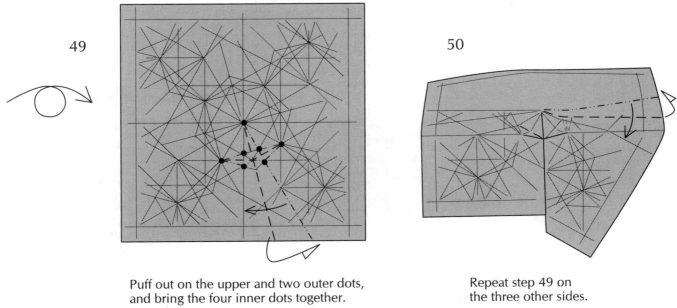

49

Puff out on the upper and two outer dots,
and bring the four inner dots together.

50

Repeat step 49 on
the three other sides.

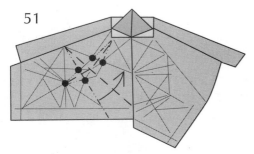

51

At the top is a pyramid on a square. Puff out on the left dot and bring the four inner dots together. This is similar to step 49.

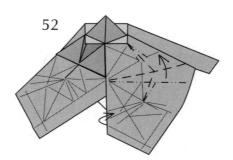

52

Repeat step 51 on the right while sliding the paper at the bottom center.

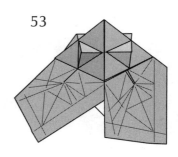

53

Repeat steps 51–52 all around.

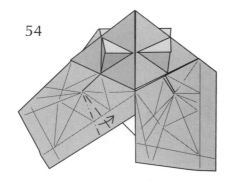

54

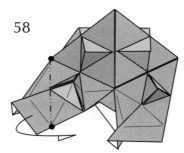

55

Fold behind and form a straight line between the dots.

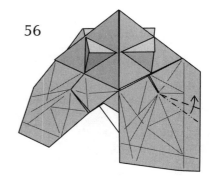

56

Repeat steps 54–55 on the three other sides.

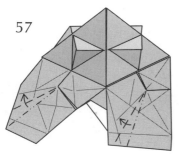

57

Repeat on the other two sides.

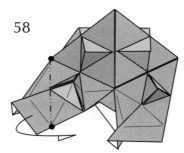

58

Fold behind and form a straight line between the dots. Repeat on the three other sides.

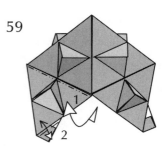

59

Fold and unfold twice. Repeat all around.

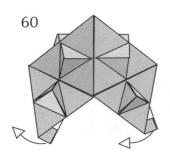

60

Unfold. Repeat all around.

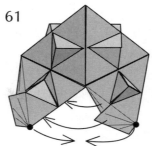

61

Bring the for corners (two shown) together at the bottom and tuck the tabs. The four bottom tabs form a twist lock.

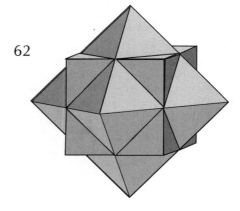

62

Gamma Star